IRISH HUM

Favourit

2 : *

150 : 4

150 : 14   47 : 4

81 : 3   47 : 9

33 : 1   47 : 12 .

46 : 9

IRISH
HUMOROUS
QUOTATIONS

Edited by
Laurence Flanagan

GILL & MACMILLAN

Published in Ireland by
Gill & Macmillan Ltd
Goldenbridge
Dublin 8
with associated companies throughout the world
© Selection of texts Laurence Flanagan 1994

0 7171 2136 4

Design and print origination by
O'K Graphic Design, Dublin

Printed by
ColourBooks Ltd, Dublin

A catalogue record is available for this book from the British Library.

1 3 5 4 2

Dedicated to the memory of
my friend
John Maloney, of Carrick, Co. Donegal
who died 28 February 1994

Contents

Introduction

The distinction between 'wit' and 'humour' is an elusive one; Cyril Cusack, in his *The Humour is on Me*, was probably not the first to suggest that 'whereas wit, of that special brand precious and peculiar to the Irish intelligence, is largely motivated by malice, humour – less native? – may be charged with the spirit of charity'. Certainly Oliver St John Gogarty had previously suggested that 'the Irish have wit but little humour'; hopefully this collection of Irish humorous quotations gives the lie to that. Among the examples cited there are certainly examples of wit – even in the implied pejorative sense – but there are also examples of every degree of 'humour' from the kind that makes you bray with laughter to the kind that brings a rather wry smile to your lips: 'bon mots, aperçus and apophthegms', but not jokes as such. Sometimes the malice, or even cruelty, is more apparent than real, occasioned by an oportunity to turn a phrase that is apposite and amusing, even though it may not appear amusing to its subject; I myself have been accused of being 'the kind of man who would sacrifice a lifelong friendship for the sake of a well-turned insult'. It is not, however, the insult that is irresistible, it is the turning of it. This, lightly said, is perhaps one of the factors that influenced James Joyce – the temptation simply to 'turn' language, resulting in passages like 'he was down with the whopping laugh at the age of the loss of reason the whopping first time he prediseased me'.

One question that defeats me is, 'What makes humour particularly Irish?' I suspect that we ourselves are incapable of answering this, it must be left to outsiders – preferably impartial outsiders, who, if they are totally impartial probably don't have a sense of humour at all themselves. The English, for example, will frequently observe of a casually thrown off remark, 'I say, that's frightfully Irish'; but then they will say that of an Irishman drinking whiskey out of a pint tumbler – Irish whiskey of course: while we can't define it we can certainly recognise it, and, like the humour, enjoy it.

Possibly one circumstance that helps make Irish humour particularly Irish is the kind of things that happen here. Where else could a dredger, aptly named 'Bar Maid', be set adrift by vandals, thus causing the turning of the tables whereby a barmaid becomes a hazard to seamen? This precisely happened early in 1994, at Ballycastle, Co. Antrim.

There is, too, a distinguished antiquity to Irish humour, not only in the simple, rather 'schoolboy' humour of the Táin, but also throughout the centuries and exemplified in Irish proverbs, where, hopefully, the existence of an Irish form validates the Irish origin, as, for example, in 'Though honey is sweet do not lick it off the briar' (Ma's mils a mhil, ná ligh-sa de'n dréaoig i).

Irish humour 'travels' well; on a recent visit to Amsterdam I observed the following in Mulligan's, one of the many Irish bars (many are owned by Dutchmen, which is probably another sort of Irish joke) in that delightful city: 'God created whiskey to keep the Irish from ruling the world.' How stomach-churningly true this is – and surely proof, if any was needed, that the Irish can laugh at themselves.

It is also true that Irish humour is so universally recognised that the well-known (and well-turned) quotation from *Ulysses,* 'Greater love than this, he said, no man hath that a man lay down his wife for his friend' was avidly used by the British press of Brigadier Parker-Bowles, when, apparently, he did just that.

In compiling this selection I am more than usually grateful and obligated to Fergal Tobin, who introduced me to several humorists of whom I was unaware, and helped me through the over-charted waters of James Joyce; like (in this respect) Oliver St John Gogarty I only went to Oxford, because, presumably, I was not clever enough for Trinity, Dublin, and therefore incapable of understanding James Joyce.

Muster and Index of Authors and Perpetrators

Anonymous

1. I love every food that begins with 'A', anchovies, artichokes, asparagus, alcohol – Anything, in fact.

2. The principle advantage of a woman's having small breasts is that they stay where you left them, more or less.

3. Sermons – and religious broadcasts – have become so boring that you would expect the universal anthem to be 'Tedium laudamus'.

4. When I was stroking my college eight I could strike a felicitous and appropriate rate more quickly and expertly than any County Council.

5. They say that radio broadcasting involves sound waves – all I can say from some of the programmes I have heard recently is that large numbers of unsound waves have crept in.

6. We watched the Scottish Fiddle Orchestra performing superbly in the Ulster Hall – with large numbers of respectable middle-aged people reeling in the aisles. Funnily had it been called the Irish Fiddle Orchestra they wouldn't have behaved like that, for the simple reason that they wouldn't have been there.

7. Those yelling drunkards who woke me in the middle of the night should be transported to some distant colony for sleep-stealing.

8. He put all his women on pedestals – probably so that he could look up their skirts.

9. When all is said and done sexual intercourse is the only thing worth a fuck.

10. If love really was merely sexual attraction or lust how different our portrait galleries would be.

11. A God by any other name is just as nimble with thunder-bolts.

12. Under no circumstances will breakfast be served after lunch. *Notice in Co. Clare hotel*

13. Here lies a famous belly-slave,
Whose mouth was wider than his grave:
Reader tread lightly o'er his sod,
For, should he gape, you're gone,
By God.
Grave inscription at Rathgraffe, Co. Meath

14. Atá ben istír
Ní abraim a ainm
maidid essi a deilm
amal chloich a tailm.

(There's a woman in the land
I won't mention her name –
And when she breaks wind,
It's like a stone from a sling.)
in *Dictionary of Irish Quotations* by S. Sheehan

1. [Attributed to a Kerry Member of Parliament in respect of a local landlord] 'So rapacious is he that if you placed him on an uninhabited island, within half an hour he would have his hands in the pockets of the naked savages.'
in *Letters and Leaders of My Day* by Timothy Healy

2. [Attributed to an elderly priest on being asked why there were no Jesuits in the Cork Diocese] 'I attribute that, Mr Healy, to the power of prayer.'
in *Letters and Leaders of My Day* by Timothy Healy

3. Ro-ordaigh Moling proinn mbig dhó frisin ré sin, doigh adubairt re bhanchoig ni do bhleaghan na mbó do thabairt dó. Muirghil a hainm-sidhe, as í ba ben do Mhungán do mhuicidhi Moling. Ba hí méd na proinni sin dobheiredh an bhen dó .i. nodhingedh a sáil conuige a hadhronn isin mbualtrach fa coimhnesa dhi agus nofágbadh a lán lemnachta ann do Suibhne.

(Moling ordered a collation for him at that hour, for he told his cook to give him some of each day's milking. Muirghil was her name; she was wife of Mongan, swineherd to Moling. This was the extent of the meal the woman used to give him; she used to thrust her heel up to her ankle in the cowdung nearest her and leave the full of it of new milk there for Suibhne.)
Buile Suibhne

4. 'A popa Lugaid, inim áigetar-sa in tslúaig?'
'Tongu do dia,' or Lugaid, 'ní laimethar óenfer ná días úadib tabairt a fúail i n-imechtur in dúnaid mani bet fíchtib nó tríchtaib.'

('O friend Lugaid, do the army hold me in fear?'
'I swear by the god of my people,' said Lugaid, 'that not one man or two dare go outside the camp to make water unless they go in companies of twenty or thirty.')
Táin Bó Cúailnge

5. 'Mad dia ngona,' ol Medb, 'is búaid. Gid hé gontair and dano, is dingbáil tromma don tslóg. Ní réid bith fris im longud nó im ligi.'

('If he kills Cú Chulainn,' said Medb, 'it means victory. If he is himself killed, it will be a relief to the host. It is not pleasant to consort with Cúr eating and sleeping.')
Táin Bó Cúailnge

6. Haenri Amreigh h. Neill, saigh n-eini agus n-eagnama agus fear claen coirpi colach, d'eg sa bliadhain-sea.

(Énrí Aimhréidh ó Néill, renowned for hospitality and valour, an unjust, wicked, and sinful man, died this year.)
Miscellaneous Annals

7. 'Now that they have voted Sinn Féin we must tell them what Sinn Féin is.'
in *The Life Story of Éamon de Valera* by Sean O'Faolain

Richard
Adams

1. 'You have now been acquitted by a Limerick jury, and you may now leave the dock without any other stain upon your character.'
in *The Old Munster Circuit* by Maurice Healy

2. 'I cannot stand his lectures,' said one. 'Yes,' said another, 'his speeches are as long as his fingernails.' 'Ah! but not so much in them!'
in *The Old Munster Circuit* by Maurice Healy

Dave
Allen

3. Don't mourn for me now
Don't mourn for me never
I'm going to do nothing
For ever and ever.
His own suggested epitaph

4. If John Major was drowning, his whole life would pass in front of him and he wouldn't be in it.
The Independent, March 1993

Éamonn
Andrews

5. I went for a walk the other day in Howth and although it was quite crowded with people I found that Gay was stopped more often than I was. I didn't get a second look from some of them. It didn't bother me.
in *Éamonn Andrews: His Life* by Gus Smyth

6. They don't treat me as a star in Ireland, just someone who turns up in their homes from time to time.
in *Éamonn Andrews: His Life* by Gus Smyth

John
Banville

7. We clasped hands and danced together, and Wackher's little dog, which he had brought with him, ran about in circles barking shrilly, until, overcome by our hilarity and quite beside itself, it jumped up and clasped me amorously about the leg, as dogs will, licking its lips and insanely grinning, which made us laugh the harder.
Kepler

8. It has always been my habit to praise what, in my opinion, others have done well. Never do I scorn other people's work because of jealousy, never do I belittle others' knowledge when I lack it myself. Likewise I never forget myself when I have done something better, or discovered something sooner.
Kepler

9. He, who had been such a brilliant student, detested teaching. In his classes he experienced a weird frustration.

The lessons he had to expound were always, always just somewhere off to the side of what really interested him, so that he was forever holding himself in check, as a boatman presses a skiff against the run of the river. The effort exhausted him, left him sweating and dazed. Frequently the rudder gave way, and he was swept off helplessly on the flood of his enthusiasm, while his poor dull students stood abandoned on the receding bank, waving weakly.
Kepler

1. I even found my way into a brothel in the Piraeus, where the fat madam (why are they always fat?) welcomed me with a wide smile and a flood of incoherent, though entertaining English; I declined to have her fit me in, as she so aptly put it.
Nightspawn

2. By the way, what an odd formulation that is: to get life. Words so rarely mean what they mean.
The Book of Evidence

3. He really did try to believe in this fantasy of a great good place that had been taken away from us and our kind – our kind being Castle Catholics, as he liked to say, yes, sir, Castle Catholics, and proud of it! But I think there was less pride than chagrin. I think he was secretly ashamed not to be a Protestant: he would have had so much less explaining, so much less justifying to do.
The Book of Evidence

4. Madmen do not frighten me, or even make me uneasy. Indeed, I find that their ravings soothe me. I think it is because everything, from the explosion of a nova to the fall of dust in a deserted room, is to them of vast and equal significance, and therefore meaningless.
The Book of Evidence

Sir Jonah
Barrington

5. 'Don't you know me, Barrington? Why don't you speak to me?'
'Tis because I do know you that I do not speak to you,' replied my son.
Personal Sketches

6. The brains and tongues of the Irish are somehow differently formed or furnished from those of other people.
Personal Sketches

7. An Irish inn has been an eternal subject of ridicule to every writer upon the habits and appearances of my native country.
Personal Sketches

8. . . . understood books and wine better than any of the party, had all his days treated money so extremely ill, that it would continue no longer in his service.
Personal Sketches

John
Bartley

1. 'Is there any question of religion in this case, Mr Bartley?' 'No religion at all, my Lord; all the parties are Presbyterians!'
in *The Old Munster Circuit* by Maurice Healy

Brendan
Behan

2. A general and a bit of shooting makes you forget your troubles . . . it takes your mind off the cost of living.
The Hostage

3. When I came back to Dublin, I was courtmartialled in my absence and sentenced to death in my absence, so I said they could shoot me in my absence.
The Hostage

4. I wish I'd been a mixed infant.
The Hostage

5. PAT: He was an Anglo-Irishman.
MEG: In the blessed name of God, what's that?
PAT: A Protestant with a horse.
The Hostage

6. It's the H bomb. It's such a big bomb it's got me scared of the little bombs.
The Hostage

7. An Anglo-Irishman only works at riding horses, drinking whiskey and reading double-meaning books in Irish at Trinity College.
The Hostage

8. OFFICER: The loss of liberty is a terrible thing.
PAT: That's not the worst thing, nor the redcaps, nor the screws. Do you know what the worst thing is?
OFFICER: No.
PAT: The other Irish patriots in along with you.
The Hostage

9. TERESA: It's because of the English being in Ireland that he fought.
SOLDIER: And what about the Irish in London? Thousands of them. Nobody's doing anything to them. We just let them drink their way through it.
The Hostage

10. PAT: Him a general? He's a messenger boy. He's not fit to be a batman.
MEG: I've heard they're all generals nowadays.
PAT: Like their mothers before them.
The Hostage

11. Some time ago there was a famine in this country and people were dying all over the place. Well, your Queen Victoria, or whatever her bloody name was, sent five pounds to the famine

fund and at the same time she sent five pounds to the Battersea Dogs' Home so no one could accuse her of having rebel sympathies.
The Hostage

1. MISS GILCHRIST: Oh, Miss Meg, I repulse your prognostications. It would answer you better to go and clean your carpet.
MEG: How dare you? When I was ill I lay prostituted on that carpet. Men of good taste have complicated me on it.
The Hostage

2. There was a party to celebrate Deirdre's return from her abortion in Bristol.
After the Wake

3. The Fianna Fáil crowd recognised but the one true Pope, by the name of Éamon de Valera, late of 42nd St.
After the Wake

4. 'All right,' said Maria, with resignation, 'if you say so, I'll make conversation with them.'
   'You'll do as you're fucking well told,' said he, in Castilian.
After the Wake

5. She was never sure, she said, what religion I was. The old cow, and all belonging to me Catholics since 432 AD. But I knew fish was scarce and not good that week, so I said I was a Protestant, and she gave me steak.
After the Wake

6. He was a genuine religious man, and one of the few religious men that was not a worse bastard than ordinary people.
After the Wake

7. He was a humble and simple soul, and only told lies in the way of business, to get a drink, a feed or the price of his keep.
After the Wake

8. It was suspected that some of them took piano lessons and dancing lessons while we of the North Circular Road took anything we could lay our hands on which was not nailed down.
After the Wake

9. I'd have let a few shouts at *The Playboy* myself, on the first night, only for, (i), I wasn't present, and (ii), the play is good gas.
After the Wake

10. The English and the Americans dislike only *some* Irish – the same Irish that the Irish themselves detest, Irish writers – the ones that *think*.
Richard's Cork Leg

11. Other people have a nationality. The Irish and the Jews have a psychosis.
Richard's Cork Leg

12. Killing your wife is a natural class of a thing that could happen to the best of us.
The Quare Fellow

1. DUNLAVIN: Do you know who feels it worse going out to be topped?
PRISONER A: Corkmen and Northerners . . . they've such bloody hard necks.
The Quare Fellow

2. There's only one brand of tobacco allowed here – 'Three Nuns'. None today, none tomorrow, and none the day after.
The Quare Fellow

3. Ah, when all is said and done, he's someone's rearing after all, he could be worse, he could be a screw or an official from the Department.
The Quare Fellow

4. HEALEY: Well, we have one consolation, Regan, the condemned man gets the priest and the sacraments, more than his victim got maybe. I venture to suggest that some of them die holier than if they had finished their natural span.
WARDER REGAN: We can't advertise 'Commit a murder and die a happy death,' sir. We'd have them all at it. They take religion very seriously in this country.
The Quare Fellow

5. You're the life of the party, aren't you? You remind me of the little girl who was sent in to cheer her father up. She was so good at it that he cut his throat.
The Quare Fellow

6. The Belfast IRA got so many rifles from Ballykinlar, they used to call it the Stores.
Borstal Boy

7. KEN: Some people don't like the Irish – I do.
BRENDAN: We're very popular among ourselves.
Borstal Boy

8. Ken they never would accept. In a way, as the middle class and the upper class in England spend so much money and energy in maintaining the difference between themselves and the working class, Ken was only getting what his people paid for.
Borstal Boy

9. They used to 'ave religious texts on the wall of the condemned cell in Durham that Chaplain 'ad put there. One of them said, 'Today is the morrow you worried about yesterday and nothing's 'appened'. It was the last thing a bloke saw as 'e went out to be hanged.
Borstal Boy

10. Ná thrácht ar an mhinistéir Ghallda,
Ná ar a chreideamh gán bheann, gán bhrí,
Mar níl mar bhuan-chloch dá teampuill,
Ach magairle Annraoi, Rí.

(Don't speak of the alien minister, Nor of his Church without

meaning nor faith,
For the foundation stone of his
  temple
Is the ballocks of Henry the
  Eighth!)
Borstal Boy

1. Now, Borstal is a lovely place,
At nighttime there they wash
  your face.
'Good night, my son,' the screw
  will say,
'There ends another happy day!'
There's a screw to tuck you into
  bed,
And lay a pillow 'neath your head.
And as you lie there fast asleep,
'E'll plant a kiss right on your
  cheek!
Borstal Boy

2. They're not working-class
blokes. They're reared up to
thieving and stealing and living
off prostitutes the same as the
boss class.
Borstal Boy

3. TOM: 'Aven't you noticed nearly
all thieves are Tories?
BRENDAN: Maybe it's because all
Tories are thieves.
Borstal Boy

4. In Ireland, down the country
anyway, if a girl got put up the
pole she might as well leave on
the next boat or drown herself
and have done with it. The people
there are so Christian and easily
shocked.
Borstal Boy

5. I took me girl up to the zoo
To show her the lion and the
  kangaroo
All she wanted to see was me oul'
  cockatoo
Up in the zoological gardens.
Borstal Boy

6. We're all good kids. We're all
the kids our mothers warned us
against.
Borstal Boy

7. TERESA: Well, I've always heard
that de Valera is a wonderful man.
They say he's fluent in seven
languages.
PATRICK: More's the pity we can't
understand him once in a while.
An Giall

8. Not that the Horse-Protestants
were any better, but they were
longer at it. They were just as
ignorant except that their ill-
manners are sharpened by time.
Brendan Behan's Island

9. 'Anything in the paper this
morning, Julia?'
  'Nothing, Mary, only the Pope
is trying to make peace.'
  'God forgive him, it's a wonder
he wouldn't mind his own
interference. It's enough to make
you turn Protestant.'
Brendan Behan's Island

10. I don't know many working
writers in Ireland because there
aren't many. There are civil
servants, spoiled priests waiting

to be rehabilitated, judges, ex-convicts, retired nuns and escaped agriculturalists who write: but these are only honorary screevenorai.
Brendan Behan's Island

1. I often heard that Cork people were clever but if a lunatic can go around with fifty or sixty pounds stuck in his coat, what must the sane people be like?
Brendan Behan's Island

2. I believe they manage things better across the other side. Sure God help the Irish, if it was raining soup, they'd be out with forks.
Brendan Behan's Island

3. I'm not a communist. I'm too humble and modest. The communists want to free all the workers of the world. I'm content to make a start and free one member of it at a time . . . myself.
Brendan Behan's Island

4. They don't apparently care about people being drunk in the Navy which is uncommon civil of them and to their lasting credit.
Brendan Behan's Island

Dominic
Behan

5. Parable recalled the excitement of the confessional. He remembered as a kid wanking when he felt there wasn't enough

sin in his week to earn a proper penance.
The Public World of Parable Jones

6. All changed now since rationalism had taken all the sin out of masturbation, and the Hierarchy commanded a sublimation of sex. Changed utterly: a terrible beauty was bored.
The Public World of Parable Jones

7. Rumour has it that Harry McGill of McGill and Gill, publishers, cannot read. In a profession where simple accountancy is preferable to a degree in English, illiteracy is not considered to be a great drawback.
The Public World of Parable Jones

Sam Hanna
Bell

8. He had come to the conclusion that Nature, with her continual and invariably indiscreet fertility, was a bad example to simple folk.
December Bride

George
Berkeley

9. This island is a region of dreams and trifles.
The Querist

Maeve
Binchy

1. At the end of a long night he suggested she come back to his room for a drink. Julia was about to agree when she suddenly realised with a horrible shock that she literally didn't know how to do it.
London Transports

2. It's harder than you think to find somebody to sleep with you, in a limited time, and for a limited time and with no strings, and with no build-up.
London Transports

3. Everyone knew that Daphne's friend Mike was a shit and to give us our due most of us said so.
London Transports

4. 'Are you shuddering at me or is that passion?' he asked.
   'Unbridled passion,' she said, wondering was it normal to lie beside the most attractive man in London and think not of him but of the sitting room wall back in the family home.
Silver Wedding

5. The Bishop was a thin silent man. He didn't walk to places but was more inclined to glide. Under his long soutane or his regal style vestments he might well have had wheels rather than feet. He had already said he would like to process rather than drive from the railway station to the school.

Very nice if you were a gliding person and it was a cool day.
The Copper Beech

6. 'When I was young I'd never seen a squirrel,' Father Barry said. 'Only in picture books, and there was a giraffe on the same page so I always thought they were the same size. I was terrified of meeting one.'
The Copper Beech

7. Mrs Ryan had always thought that if the whole wealth of the world was taken back and divided out equally, giving the same amount to each person, you'd find in five years that the same people would end up having money and power and the same people would end up shiftless and hopeless. In a changing world, she found this view very comforting.
The Copper Beech

8. Eddie had hair that grew upwards from his head. Foxy Dunne had said he looked like a lavatory brush. Eddie didn't know what a lavatory brush was. They didn't have one in their house, but when he saw one in Ryan's Hotel he was very annoyed. His hair wasn't as bad as that.
The Copper Beech

9. If you were nice to girls, if you smiled at them and listened to them, just liked them, they opened up like flowers.
The Copper Beech

George A.
Birmingham

1. The wife who pays her husband's debts for him has a hold over him ever afterwards.
The Search Party

2. Being an Englishwoman, she held the curious theory that the police exist for the protection of the public.
The Search Party

3. It's your ordinary, well-behaved woman who drives a man perfectly frantic if he has any spirit in him.
The Search Party

4. I should say we are now practically certain that there hasn't been an accident – at all events not a bicycle accident. I've had seventeen bicycle accidents in my time, and my experience is that the machine is always far more injured than the rider.
The Major's Niece

5. If you think that I'm the sort of man who'd give improper books to a girl you're utterly mistaken. As a matter of fact I don't read books that have anything objectionable in them myself, except the ancient Fathers of the Church.
The Major's Niece

6. There are still to be found in Ireland several towns of great importance, in the opinion of their inhabitants, which are twenty miles or more distant from any railway station.
The Major's Niece

7. 'You were a slip of a girl with a sharp tongue when I mind you first, and a woman with a sharp tongue when I said good-bye to you. You have lost your bonny looks and your shining red hair; you've lost your husband, so you tell me, but you haven't lost your tongue.'
The Northern Iron

8. It is noticeable that women with sharp tongues are generally more efficient than their gentler sisters.
The Northern Iron

Dermot
Bolger

9. Cute country girls in their bedsits. They may have lost their virginity but they'll probably still have the box it came in.
The Journey Home

10. Before the last election, Plunkett and two of his election workers are up in the cemetery at midnight registering people for the vote. Patrick's writing down this yellow fellow's name he's after coming across who used to own the Chinese take-away in the village. 'Ah, Jasus, Patrick,' says

one of the workers, 'he's not even Irish.' Plunkett looks up indignant and says, 'We'll have no racism here. He's as much right to vote as anyone else in this cemetery.'
The Journey Home

1. A gruff fucker with a goat, scruffy from the filth of the roads. Patric or Patraigh or some such name, prophesying out of him down by the stream. His three gods that form the one god, his riddles and his trickery. Too many bloody foreigners pass this way and this blow-in not even bothering to hawk or trade with us. His own scrawny goat given to him by some raggedy king up in the arse of Tara. The gods would piss on you if you sacrificed the like of it to them.
The Woman's Daughter

Dion
Boucicault

2. COOL: If Sir Harcourt knew this, he would go mad, he would discharge me.
YOUNG COURTLY: You flatter yourself; that would be no proof of his insanity.
London Assurance

3. MAX: I'm as grey as an old badger, or a wild rabbit; while you are – are as black as a young rook. I say, whose head grew your hair, eh?
London Assurance

4. Wine and love are the only two indescribable things in nature; but I prefer the wine, because its consequences are not entailed and are more easily got rid of.
London Assurance

5. I have ascertained for a fact, that every tradesman of mine lives with his wife, and thus you see it has become a vulgar and plebeian custom.
London Assurance

6. A husband six thousand miles off is the same thing as none at all.
The Corsican Brothers

7. KINCHELA: I don't know why one of these girls didn't introduce me.
MOLINEUX: They paid me the compliment of presuming that I had no desire to form your acquaintance.
The Shaughraun

Andrew
Boyd

8. I find no pleasure in presenting this book to the public because it is the profile of a person who, no matter how much he may represent the views of the narrow-minded Unionists in the constituency of East Down, could hardly be regarded as fit to be a Prime Minister, even of so miserable a place as Northern Ireland.
Brian Faulkner

1. I have searched through official documents and through the files of many newspapers but in none of them could I find where Faulkner had ever said a kindly word about anyone.
Brian Faulkner

Robert Boyle

2. He that said it was not good for man to be alone, placed the celibate amongst the inferior states of perfection.
Works

Joseph Brady

3. 'When I was a chap they blamed the new wheel-ploughs for the bad weather.'
In Monavalla

4. 'Who would want to discuss immortality when he is sober?'
In Monavalla

5. There is a puritan streak in the Americans. They sometimes appear to me as not yet quite grown-up; they are like young giants on their good behaviour in an academy for young ladies.'
In Monavalla

6. That same gent has a one-track mind and the traffic on it is very light.
In Monavalla

7. 'They hadn't a shilling between them, so they tossed up a sledge-hammer. If it stopped in the sky, they'd stay at home; if it came down, they'd go.'
In Monavalla

Fr Pat Buckley

8. I'm the Red Adair of the Catholic Church in Ireland. I deal with the marital blow-outs.
The Irish Times, May 1993

Edmund Burke

9. Men who undertake considerable things, even in a regular way, ought to give us ground to presume ability.
Reflections on the Revolution in France

10. People will not look forward to prosperity, who never look backwards to their ancestors.
Reflections on the Revolution in France

11. No man can mortgage his injustice as a pawn for his fidelity.
Reflections on the Revolution in France

12. But what is liberty without wisdom, and without virtue? It is the greatest of all possible evils; for it is folly, vice, and madness without intuition or restraint.
Reflections on the Revolution in France

1. Kings will be tyrants from policy, when subjects are rebels from principle.
Reflections on the Revolution in France

2. Whilst shame keeps its watch, virtue is not wholly extinguished in the heart.
Reflections on the Revolution in France

3. All men that are ruined, are ruined on the side of their natural propensities.
About William Pitt

4. I am convinced that we have a degree of delight, and that no small one, in the real misfortunes and pains of others.
The Sublime and the Beautiful

5. Example is the school of mankind, and they will learn at no other.
On a Regicide Peace

6. So then because some towns in England are not represented, America is to have no representation at all. They are 'our children'; but when children ask for bread we are not to give a stone.
Speech on American Taxation

7. When we speak of the commerce with our colonies, fiction lags after truth, invention is unfruitful, and imagination cold and barren.
Speech on Conciliation with the Colonies

8. There is however a limit at which forebearance ceases to be a virtue.
Observations on a Late Publication on the Present State of the Nation

9. The writers against religion, whilst they oppose every system, are wisely careful never to set up any of their own.
A Vindication of Natural Society

Gay
Byrne

10. If you can have an exaltation of larks (or a fluff of radio announcers), this was a constipation of a 'Late Late Show'.
The Time of My Life

11. Oliver Reed does not come on to a show, he makes an entrance. In my case I took one look into his eyes and realised there was nobody home.
The Time of My Life

12. The more splendiferous the monument erected by wife to husband's memory in those days, the more it would be a memorial to their unity in life and the greater the retrospective status of the marriage.
The Time of My Life

1. As often happens when widows are released from domesticity, the two of them began to have a whale of a time.
The Time of My Life

2. Eventually, courtship serious, the day came when I was to meet this man.
'How do you do?'
'Fine, thank you, Mr Watkins. How do *you* do?'
'Fine. Will you have a drink?'
'No, Mr Watkins, I don't drink . . .'
'Will you have a smoke, then?'
'No, thank you, Mr Watkins, I don't smoke . . .'
(Pause) 'Ah, musha, why doesn't God call you!'
The Time of My Life

Patrick
Campbell

3. 'I got an uprush of aesthetic disgust,' I said. 'I sent them all off to be reframed.' He considered this for a while. 'I always thought the frames were fine,' he said. 'You'd have done better to have them repictured.'
All Ways on Sundays

4. Singing in public-houses, whether subsidised by the Arts Council or left to the whim of the individual performer, is an insupportable affront to the comfort of the other customers.
All Ways on Sundays

5. Song-fests of this kind are conducted in what we music-lovers call the eight-pint pitch, or key of G, where G stands for gallon. It begins a little too high for the leader himself to see through to the end and is lowered by each successive chorister until it achieves a level of raucous bawling, acceptable to all, that will see us out until closing time.
All Ways on Sundays

6. I lived in Ireland on and off for thirty years, and for another twenty in England, and I believe I always had the feeling at the back of my mind of being trapped. Aer Lingus regret to announce that due to fog all flights are cancelled until further notice, or owing to a technical hitch among the baggage porters all BEA planes will be grounded until the end of time.
Gullible Travels

7. What kind of holiday can you take when you live in almost continual sunshine in an olive grove in the mountains, which is only twenty minutus away from the beaches and the sea?
Gullible Travels

8. I've got difficult feet. They're almost round, like an elephant's. Lengthways they're size ten and sideways size twelve.
Gullible Travels

1. I slipped a vodka into my tomato juice, as a weight reducer, and then added Worcester sauce, pepper and was about to reach for the salt when I remembered something in Doctor's diet sheet that urged me to go easy on the salt as it was a water-retainer.
The Coarse of Events

2. Upon finding our publisher already aboard, in place of the cascade of bitterness, accusation, derision and complaint which forms so much of the normal communication between publishers and authors, we even said good morning to him, too, and he replied in like terms quite civilly.
The Coarse of Events

3. False Verbena, however, proved tougher work. The jade has a smell of verbena, but coarsened beyond measure, putting one in mind of Dorian Gray on a bad night.
The Coarse of Events

William
Carleton

4. Inasmuch as the moral and intellectual organs of Irishmen predominate over the physical and sensual, the people ought therefore to be ranked at the very tip-top of morality.
An Essay on Irish Swearing

5. We would warn the phrenologists, however, not to be too sanguine in drawing inferences from an examination of Paddy's head. Heaven only knows the scenes in which it is engaged, and the protuberances created by a long life of hard fighting. Many an organ and development is brought out on it by the cudgel, that never would have appeared had Nature been left to herself.
An Essay on Irish Swearing

6. Drinking, fighting and swearing are the three great characteristics of every people. Paddy's love of fighting and of whiskey has long been proverbial; and of his tact in swearing much has also been said.
An Essay on Irish Swearing

7. He is not, however, totally averse to facts; but, like your true poet, he veils, changes and modifies them with such skill that they possess all the merit and graces of fiction.
An Essay on Irish Swearing

8. Although there is much laxity of principle among Irishmen, naturally to be expected from men whose moral state has been neglected by the legislature, and deteriorated by political and religious asperity, acting upon quick passions and badly regulated minds – yet we know that they possess, after all, a strong but vague, undirected sense of devotional feeling and reverence, which are associated with great crimes and dark shades of character.
An Essay on Irish Swearing

1. It is not in Ireland with criminals as in other countries, where the character of a murderer or incendiary is notoriously bad, as resulting from a life of gradual profligacy and villainy. Far from it. In Ireland you will find these crimes perpetrated by men who are good fathers, good husbands, good sons and good neighbours – by men who would share their last morsel or their last shilling with a fellow-creature in distress – who would generously lose their lives for a man who had obliged them, provided he had not incurred their enmity – and who would protect a defenceless stranger as far as lay in their power.
An Essay on Irish Swearing

2. Paddy, when engaged in a fight, is never at a loss for a weapon, and we may also affirm that he is never at a loss for an oath.
An Essay on Irish Swearing

3. Could society hold together a single day if nothing but truth were spoken? Would not law and lawyers soon become obsolete if nothing but truth were sworn? What would become of Parliament if truth alone were uttered there? Its annual proceedings might be despatched in a month.
An Essay on Irish Swearing

4. Fiction is the basis of society, the bond of commercial prosperity, the channel of communication between nation and nation, and not unfrequently the interpreter between a man and his own conscience.
An Essay on Irish Swearing

5. There is compassion for the peculiar state of the poor boy who perhaps only burnt a family on their beds; benevolence to prompt the generous effort in his behalf; disinterestedness to run the risk of becoming an involuntary absentee; fortitude in encountering a host of brazen-faced lawyers; patience under the unsparing grip of a cross-examiner; perseverance in conducting the oath to its close against a host of difficulties; and friendship which bottoms and crowns them all.
An Essay on Irish Swearing

6. Phelim then sat down to breakfast – for he was one of those happy mortals whose appetite is rather sharpened by affliction.
Phelim O'Toole's Courtship

7. He happened to be one of those men who can conceal nothing when in a state of intoxication. Whenever he indulged in liquor too freely, the veil which discretion had drawn over their recriminations was put aside, and a dolorous history of their weaknesses, doubts, hopes and wishes most unscrupulously given to every person on whom the complainant could fasten. When sober he had no recollection of this, so that many a conversation of cross-purposes

took place between him and his neighbours with reference to the state of his domestic inquietude and their want of children.
Phelim O'Toole's Courtship

Sir Edward Carson

1. 'I do not care twopence whether it is treason or not.'
in *The Life Story of Éamon de Valera* by Sean O'Faolain

Frank Cassells

2. Al Capone was not caught for racketeering or the movement of illicit booze. He was caught for income-tax evasion. We don't care how we catch them, but catch them we will.
The Irish Times, March 1993

Austin Clarke

3. Men elbow their counter in public-houses, drink
Their pints of plain, their chaser, large or small one,
Talk in the snug, the lounge, nod gravely, wink fun
In meanings, argue, treat one another, swallow
The fume, the ferment. Joyful, self-important,
Soon all are glorious, all are immortal

Beings of greater days, hierophants . . .
Guinness was bad for me

4. . . . sent a young fellow, with shirt-tails flying the flag
Of his country, in search of bare toes and a shawl as bedraggled.
But how could he marry? His only belongings were longings,
Hugs, squeezes, kisses, a hundred thousand strong.
Poems and Satires

5. Moral training in Ireland is severe and lasts until marriage. Even in childhood we are taught by the pious clergy to battle against bad thoughts, so that we may preserve our holy purity. In youth we learn the dangers of idle talk, the temptations of self-sin, the need for avoiding stories that incite passion. For passion in Ireland is denounced as evil and obscene. Women are the snares set for us by the Devil. Even to think of a woman's body with pleasure is a mortal sin.
The Bright Temptation

6. Lovers forgot on the mountain-side
The stern law of the clergy.
The Lucky Coin

7. . . . when our dread of the unseen
Has rifled hold and corner
How shall we praise the men that freed us
From everything but thought.
The Lucky Coin

1. Burn Ovid with the rest. Lovers will find
A hedge-school for themselves and learn by heart
All that the clergy banish from the mind,
When hands are joined and head bows in the dark.
Penal Law

John
Cole

2. [of John Major] Leadership is leasehold, not freehold.
Sunday Mirror, October 1993

George
Colley

3. People can now produce evidence to justify their cynicism and their low opinion of politicians.
in *The Boss* by Joyce and Murtagh

Pádraic
Colum

4. Oh, if you ask not for me,
But leave me here instead,
The petticoat in dye-pot here
Will never fast its red.
The Poet's Circuit

5. It's my fear that my wake won't be quiet,
Nor my wake-house a silent place:
For who would keep back the hundreds
Who would touch my breast and my face?
The Poet's Circuit

6. And what to me is Gael or Gall?
Less than the Latin or the Greek –
I teach these by the dim rush-light
In smoky cabins night and weak.
But what avails my teaching slight?
Years hence, in rustic speech, a phrase,
As in wild earth a Grecian vase!
The Poet's Circuit

7. I lifted up
A scrap of paper, and saw lines upon it
Made by a quill, and saw they were in Latin,
And knew them Virgil's by their poetry
Although they were about the bulls and cows,
Their mating and the cleaning of their byres:
A Poor Scholar or a Hedge Schoolmaster
Copied from tattered book upon that page
For lads who sat here by the fireside
Generations gone: I took up other pages –
Old yellow broadsheets that were bluntly printed
And sung on streets of hangings and the like:
And there were some that were less public songs.
The Poet's Circuit

1. Back in the days when I was
   still at school,
Street songs I heard and used the
   lines I heard
Running beside my hoop as
   children's rhymes,
Not knowing that the lines came
   out of conflict
That led to prison cells,
   demolished houses.
The Poet's Circuit

2. And then and there a band
   came into life
With rebel tune that lowered
   pompousness
Of Court-house and Assize, and
   made the going
Of one man toward the gaol gate
   memorable
As though the lines of a great
   pencil showed it.
The Poet's Circuit

3. There was talk of the things
that had to be done. For death,
besides being a conclusion, is
itself an event that gives rise to
other events.
The Flying Swans

4. The Headmaster was
gentlemanly and humane; he was
able to give instruction to those
who wanted to learn something
(amongst the hundred on his
rollbook there were a few who
did).
The Flying Swans

5. Breasal was not a street child
but a road child: he was happy
going along the hedges.
The Flying Swans

6. The four of them went into a
public house opposite the Yard to
bring about that confidence and
conviviality that should attend
the initiation of a youngster into
an ancient craft.
The Flying Swans

7. My brother was told he was a
bastard, and I'm beginning to
dread how that will touch him
when he is among strange people
in strange places.'
   'I'm a bastard myself,' said
Duineen, 'and it didn't do me any
good to hear it.'
The Flying Swans

8. A dog that wanted to make its
being around and about plausible
came to him, and then, having
shown it had nothing to be
ashamed of, went back into the
shadows.
The Flying Swans

Emma
Cooke

9. Our relationship was one of
those things that happened
without much thought. Like
emigrating without bothering to
discover anything about your
destination.
Wedlocked

10. I told him that if it wasn't for
him I'd have had a proper life. I
told him that it was because I was
pregnant that I'd had to marry
Clive. The one thing, the only

thing I didn't say was the name of his actual father. (I've often wondered how Mary explained his parentage to Jesus.)
Wedlocked

1. 'The Lord giveth and the Lord taketh away,' he intoned.
   The Lord's not a mugger, it's the devil who took him away, I raged.
Wedlocked

Maurice Craig

2. If I were very rich . . . I would do all the obvious things such as cruising among the Isles of Greece and in the Baltic, and revisiting by water all those cities which must be approached by sea: Leningrad, Stockholm, Amsterdam, Genoa, Venice, Constaninople. I would go either Westwards through the Panama Canal; or Eastabout via Indonesia and Japan and would instruct my professional crew to take the ship, using the extremely precise satellite navigational aids with which she would be equipped, to the International Date Line, where I would stand on the bridge with one testicle in Wednesday and the other in Thursday. And from there I would send postcards to all my friends.
The Elephant and the Polish Question

3. Red brick in the suburb, white horse on the wall,

Eyetalian Marbles in the City Hall:
O stranger from England, why stand so aghast?
May the Lord in His mercy be kind to Belfast.

O the bricks they will bleed and the rain it will weep
And the damp Lagan fog lull the city to sleep;
It's to hell with the future and live on the past:
May the Lord in His mercy be kind to Belfast.
Ballad to a traditional refrain

Anthony Cronin

4. Anything at all, the weather or the telephone, the things that provide you with chances,
Present also the unfortunate necessity of choices,
And it is very difficult then to discover the only one who does not lie, the honestly selfish,
In the general noise and confusion of warning voices.
Collected Poems

5. Every day that knock brings its need and demand for decision,
And not to have to decide is of course to have done that about which we are sooner or later not any longer allowed to decide:
Not to have any longer to face the telephone, the train or the traffic
Is to have died.
Collected Poems

1. Take from the tales this much:
   the man who makes
A trade of thieving or of rustling
   steers
Is easy for the ranging lad to deal
   with.
The one to watch is he whom
   no-one fears.
Collected Poems

2. Now after ten days rain
The candles are stripped to their
   stalks.
Steamy as Vietnam
Ireland suspires under cloud.
The national colours, green and
   grey,
Shine eerily from earth and sky.
De Valera, the old wet blanket,
Is back in his damp park.
Collected Poems

3. The dead men in their
   comfortable chairs,
Before promotion crowned their
   smooth grey hairs,
Complained a little and
   complaining bled
Internally to death. Then got
   ahead.
Collected Poems

4. What he saw was not, of
   course, himself,
But the self who had waited her
   word in order to be
The one he had seen when he
   murmured her murmur over,
The he believed in because of
   incredible she.
Collected Poems

5. A man is ruined by his honesty:
No cover then his shivering limbs
   will drape.
Emotional cheques will be
   returned r.d.
Collected Poems

6. Count up your sins before the
   others do:
That is a little though you always
   lied,
Swearing in drink that you would
   see it through.
Collected Poems

7. Down underneath the Irish
   poor are singing
Their songs of Philadelphia in the
   morning,
Brotherly and romantically
   clinging
To those whom they would
   murder without warning.
Collected Poems

8. Every man loves the thing he
   kills and slowly
With many a tear the smiler does
   the knifing.
Collected Poems

9. The unfortunate thing about
carrying one's works about when
one is drinking is the temptation
to force them on people's
attention.
Dead as Doornails

10. Having a picture of the Queen
of England on your wall does not
amount to having a culture, a
separate culture or a cultural life.
Speaking with a South Down

accent (or a Derry or Raphoe accent) does not constitute having a cultural life. Marching twice a year behind penny whistles playing borrowed come-all-ye's in a tribal festival of hate and fear is not, in spite of all the pro-Unionist sentimentality now going on, a cultural activity worthy of a civilised man's respect: indeed it is scarcely one worthy of his other than humorous indulgence. Wearing a bowler hat on occasions of ceremony or tribal importance is not a mark of culture, superior, inferior or otherwise. There are plenty of people in the South of Ireland who wear bowler hats on occasion and you can take it from me that they are people of no culture at all.
An Irish Eye

1. He had, as has been said, friends who were not so active, unless debauchery and dissipation may be counted activities.
An Irish Eye

2. Achievement measuring is a game that all too many of us are good at; and the measurers will come from all shades of the political spectrum.
An Irish Eye

3. If you enter any of the hired and expensive warrens where the state's apparatchik are housed, the accents you will hear on the telephones in active control of your destinies, whether of high rank, and thus probably male, or

of low, and therefore more likely to be female, will be indubitably rural. If you tread even the pathways of commerce, or particularly the larger bureaucracy sort of commerce, the dulcet tones of rurality will be everywhere to be heard. Fall into the clutches of a policeman: the same thing. Be refused a drink by a publican's assistant at twenty-five past two: for the most part *idem*. Board even a bus, ditto. And so on and so forth. The Irish people, in brief, have voted with their feet. The dwellers in the most beautiful of rural surroundings have deserted them for elsewhere. Those that did not have the option of the capital, the rural proletariat, went to Birmingham, Leeds, Bradford, *et al*; but those that had the requisite political pull, knowledge of typewriting or talent for passing examinations flocked into Dublin.
An Irish Eye

4. If materialism is investing in an Audi to impress the little ladies of Leeson Street, growth is buying and eventually crashing a Mercedes to do the same. If materialism is such a blinder in Benidorm that sun and sea, indoors and out, night and day, balcony and bedroom are all one indistinguishable haze, growth is going off to repeat the performance three more times in the same year.
An Irish Eye

1. Examinations and all that surround them are such a strange, traumatic thing in Irish life that one approaches the subject with a certain amount of trepidation. In the reverence for the examination, one feels, lies, if anywhere, the heart of the matter, the key to those mysterious aspects of the Irish character which have baffled friend and foe alike. Whatever happened to the race, whatever the explanation of the contrast between the gay, anarchic Irishman of legend and the permanent and pensionable fellow he apparently all too easily becomes, the answer may lie in the eagerness with which he submits himself to a series of scholastic examinations, the reverence with which he regards the results, the almost religious awe with which he accepts them as a lifelong arbiter of ability, character and consequent happiness.
An Irish Eye

Eric
Cross

2. For many, many years, Ansty has worn, on weekdays, the same clothes, until she has become, as the Tailor describes her, 'more like a blessed bush at a holy well than a woman,' so tattered are her clothes.
The Tailor and Ansty

3. The poet's business was not to make sense but to make rhymes. Do you know that it was the poets who made all the words?
The Tailor and Ansty

4. But, as the Tailor says, he gets paid simply for being alive, sleeping or waking, in the form of his ten shillings a week pension, and he will not get any more by getting up any earlier. The rest of the people can air the world for him and put it straight before he gets up.
The Tailor and Ansty

5. The people of this country were badly and unjustly treated, and that made the hardship of their lives the more. I don't blame the English people for this. It was the English Government, and you can't judge a people by its Government. I know that the English people had to suffer the same Government, and Governments are never made of the best of a people.
The Tailor and Ansty

6. What for? Why, for no reason at all beyond the exercise of his own ingenuity. Things like that were like daisies in a bull's piss to him.
The Tailor and Ansty

7. People think that fat women are warm. I tell you that they are not. They make a damn great tunnel in the bed, and a man may as well be sleeping in a gully.
The Tailor and Ansty

1. Like all good dramatic critics, we retired to the pub across the road.
The Tailor and Ansty

2. All the schooling was in English. There wasn't a syllable of Irish. It was against the law, and you would be beat if you used it. But the people had the Irish, and good Irish too, and they spoke it amongst themselves. Now the world has changed round, and you are paid to learn it and few people have it. It's a queer state of affairs.
The Tailor and Ansty

3. We left the jury to drink itself stupid. But they could never do that if they were drinking to this day, for they were stupid before they started.
The Tailor and Ansty

4. A man can only sleep on one bed at a time. There is nothing makes food so good as hunger.
The Tailor and Ansty

5. Unlucky! It isn't half so unlucky as going to bed. Many a man had twins as the result of going to bed, and, anyway, most people die in bed.
The Tailor and Ansty

6. Of course I have a sore throat, but I wouldn't heed that at all. Why shouldn't I have a sore throat, when two public houses, and two farms of land, and mountainy land at that, have passed down my throat.
The Tailor and Ansty

7. Bad money, me foot. No money's bad money, if you have it.
The Tailor and Ansty

Edward Cuming

8. 'Moriarty saying that he had never been inside a music-hall is like Pontius Pilate boasting that he had never stolen his mother's jam.'
in *The Old Munster Circuit* by Maurice Healy

John Philpot Curran

9. [On the wit of Jeremiah Keller] 'There was no mistaking something of Keller's. The name was on the blade.'
in *John Philpot Curran* by Leslie Hale

10. A little and a peevish mind may be exasperated, but how shall it be corrected, by refutation?
in *John Philpot Curran* by Leslie Hale

11. I was in full sail to fortune, but the tempest came and nearly destroyed me, and afterwards, I was for long bearing up under jury-masts.
in *John Philpot Curran* by Leslie Hale

1. [On the Lord Chancellor
Fitzgibbon's success] 'Like a
chimney sweep, rising laboriously
through dirt and calling attention
from the roof to his surprising
elevation.'
in *John Philpot Curran* by Leslie
Hale

2. [On being asked by the Lord
Chief Justice if the meat at dinner
had been 'hung'] 'It will be if you
try it, my Lord.'
in *John Philpot Curran* by Leslie
Hale

3. An ascendancy of that form
raises to my mind a little greasy
emblem of stall-fed theology,
imported from some foreign land,
with the graces of a lady's maid,
the dignity of a side-table, the
temperance of a larder, its
sobriety the dregs of a patron's
bottle, and its wisdom the dregs
of a patron's understanding,
brought hither to devour, to
degrade, and to defame.
*Speech on Catholic
Emancipation*

4. When Saint Patrick our order
    created
And called us the Monks of the
    Screw
Good rules he revealed to our
    Abbot,
To guide us in what we should do.

But first he replenished his
    fountain
With liquor the best in the sky;

And he swore, by the word of his
    Saintship,
That fountain should never run
    dry!
*The Charter Song of the Monks of
the Screw*

Cyril
Cusack

5. Should one be anything but
deadly serious about a matter so
delicate as the 'Irish sense of
humour'?
The Humour is on Me

6. Once, for consideration by an
Irish Jesuit, rather cynically I
ventured the distinction that,
whereas wit, of that special brand
precious and peculiar to the Irish
intelligence, is largely motivated
by malice, humour – less native?
– may be charged with the spirit
of charity.
The Humour is on Me

7. I think it is an acceptable
cliché that, given a sense of
humour, man may grapple more
confidently with the moods and
tenses of life and even – in Irish
circles at any rate – that other
joker, death.
The Humour is on Me

8. Pity the man who cannot shed
a tear; more to be pitied is he who
cannot cast the shadow of a smile.
The Humour is on Me

Thomas
Davis

1. Come in the evening, or come
   in the morning,
Come when you're looked for, or
   come without warning,
Kisses and welcome you'll find
   here before you,
And the oftener you come here
   the more I'll adore you.
The Welcome

Sir Joseph
Davison

2. Any member of the Orange
Institution found frequenting
Roman Catholic public houses is
guilty of conduct unbecoming an
Orangeman and a charge to that
effect may be brought against
him and dealt with according to
our laws.
in *The Mutilation of a Nation* by
Cahir Healy

Sir John
Denham

3. Books should to one of these
   four ends conduce,
For wisdom, piety, delight, or use.
Of Prudence

Éamon
de Valera

4. 'I would remind you that I have
just as much contempt for a bully

standing or seated.'
in *The Life Story of Éamon de
Valera* by Sean O'Faolain

Vivion
de Valera

5. 'You can arrest father, but you
will never make English of us!'
in *The Life Story of Éamon de
Valera* by Sean O'Faolain

Bernadette
Devlin

6. All I did was give some money
for the buying of more barbed
wire: probably parliamentary
salary has never been better
spent.
The Price of My Soul

7. Perhaps the Reverend Ian was
right, and I perjured myself by
taking an oath of allegiance to the
British Queen.
The Price of My Soul

8. Everyone has invented their
own imaginary Bernadette
Devlins. They called me St Joan of
Arc, and St Bernadette, and the
second Messiah, and God knows
what other heresies they didn't
think of. When I turn out to be
different from the image they
have of me, they don't say 'I
formed a wrong impression of
that girl'; they are just broken-
hearted that I have 'let them
down'.
The Price of My Soul

1. I lost my temper at that meeting and told them to find another Christ to crucify, for this one was humping down off the cross.
The Price of My Soul

2. The taxi-driver's comment as he delivered me at the House one day: only two honest people had ever entered it – myself and Guy Fawkes.
The Price of My Soul

3. Who is going to put ten daggers in your back when one would do?
The Price of My Soul

4. You get more sense from the policeman at the door than from Members of Parliament, and you learn more from him about how to work the system.
The Price of My Soul

5. Nothing really matters! Parliament is just a friendly club.
The Price of My Soul

6. Because we were more or less related to half Cookstown, we had simply dozens of cousins and they all hated us.
The Price of My Soul

7. My mother was, from my point of view, despairingly Christian. You could have kicked her fifty times a day and she would still have turned the other cheek – and not just in a passive way: if you had tripped in the action of kicking her she would have lifted you up, knowing that as soon as

you got on your own two feet you were going to kick her again.
The Price of My Soul

8. Every Easter Monday there was a disagreement: my father wore the lily, and my mother protested. But after his death she always put lilies on his grave on Easter Mondays – the significance being that this was the biggest argument they ever had.
The Price of My Soul

9. It was a good farming match: he had the right breed of cows and she had the right number of pigs, and so on. So they were married, their land was amalagamated.
The Price of My Soul

10. If what I say annoys Harold Wilson it is because of his self-importance.
Evening Standard, July 1969

11. I took an oath of allegiance but I may have broken it.
Daily Telegraph, August 1969

12. It is a photograph of me breaking a brick.
The Times, October 1969

Paddy
Devlin

13. The asking for a Labour Exchange to be built on the Shankill Road is derisory. Whitelaw, to secure their co-

operation, would probably build them one in every street.
Sunday Press, July 1972

1. Merlyn Rees wrestled with his conscience and the result was a draw.
Attrib.

Polly Devlin

2. He is asked if he has actually taken a bath in his shiny new porcelain tub. He starts back in feigned alarm. 'Jaysus,' he says, 'I've hardly stuck it out on the lough for nigh on forty years to be drownded in me own front room.'
All of us there

Eilis Dillon

3. 'You're looking at my hat,' he said at last, in a creaking voice. 'I don't go out anymore, and a man must wear a hat sometimes, so I wear mine in the house. It's a good hat.'
The Lost Island

4. Then I came to a line of cottages whose doors and windows opened directly on to the road. They were all in darkness, and as I tiptoed past I heard a mighty snore from one of them. It was the snore of a man who works at his sleep, who values every moment of it.
The Lost Island

5. 'You'd never make a priest', Father Kenny said. 'Your policy is the direct opposite of the Christian idea of forebearance. Just before turning the other cheek, you would aim a clout at the persecutor's head.'
Across the Bitter Sea

6. Wherever you have shopkeepers and tradesmen, you have people that want to be well in with the police, in the hope that a few shillings will come their way, if it was only for mending their boots.
Across the Bitter Sea

Baron Richard Dowse

7. [On his opponent's apologising for an attack made erroneously] 'Mr Speaker, as the honourable gentleman has withdrawn what he has said about me, I withdraw what I was going to say about him!'
in *Letters and Leaders of My Day* by Timothy Healy

Lynn C. Doyle

8. Michael was a divil of a man for pace-makin', an' riz more rows than all in the county for all that;

for whin two dacent men had a word or two av a fair-day, maybe whin the drink was in them, an' had forgot all about it, the next day ould Michael would come round to make it up, an' wi' him mindin' them av what had passed, the row would begin worse than iver.
Ballygullion

1. The moderate men seen that both parties was makin' fools av themselves, for the place wasn't big enough for two; but moderate men are scarce in our parts, an' they could do nothin' to soothe matthers down. Whin the party work is on, it's little either side thinks av the good av thimselves or the counthry either.
Ballygullion

2. There niver should ha' been a match easier to make, an' that's just what bate it. It was too simple and complate altogether; an' the wimmen bein' the divil for pure crookedness, Susy must be carryin' on wi' wan or another, just to let Michael see he wasn't goin' to get things all his own way, till he was clane wild wi' jealousy.
Ballygullion

3. He was by way of bein' a handy man, an' always would be meddlin' at things he didn't understand. There was hardly a clock in the countryside he didn't spoil before the people found him out.
Ballygullion

4. I niver seen him frightened but wanst, an' that was whin he dhropped a shillin' in the pig-market, an' thought he wasn't goin' to find it.
Ballygullion

5. None av the polis was very fond av Billy. He was too many for them; an' nobody likes to be got the betther av, laste av all a polisman. It's more av a come-down for him than for another body.
Ballygullion

6. For an Ulster Protestant of his generation he was tolerant, though for the eternal welfare of his Roman Catholic neighbours he looked perhaps more to the mercy of their Creator than to the efficacy of their faith.
An Ulster Childhood

7. My bane brought its antidote with it. I learned to rank a good book above a good dinner; and if my sight is short, perhaps I can see more with it than some who have it longer.
An Ulster Childhood

8. If a single dog could have distinguished between the scent of a hare and of a red-herring the knowledge came through heredity and not experience.
An Ulster Childhood

9. The long line of rooks still stretches from the ploughman's heels, as if he were ploughing birds out of the earth.
An Ulster Childhood

1. As every intelligent Irishman knows, there's a close connection between porther an' hard work. A man that's workin' with his hands, an' sweatin', as he's bound to if he works at all, 'll need moisture of some kind or another, an' if there's a pleasanter way of aministherin' it than through the neck of a porther-bottle the secret hasn't leaked out, in Ireland, anyway.
Dear Ducks

2. He didn't believe in the English divil at all, but had rooted out a deal of information about another ould Gaelic chap that he thought was twice as good; though, troth, if it come to spendin' the balance of eternity with either of the two there wasn't much to choose between them.
Dear Ducks

3. Wee Mr Anthony, the solicitor, was one of them men that hasn't room in their heads for more than one idea at a time. Him bein' a solicitor, ye might think it was law his head was full of; but not a bit of it. Outside of his own office or the Petty Sessions Court, law never troubled him; he just passed his final examination an' then placed the whole business in the hands of the divil.
Dear Ducks

4. The fight, as fights do, proceeded no further than the taking off of coats. The prospective combatants were only too easily dragged apart.
Me and Mr Murphy

5. 'There's a man in Portnagree Asylum thinks his belly is made of glass,' sez I, 'an' he's sensible compared to you.'
Rosabelle

6. The general who heroically risks his men's lives is seldom cheated of victory.
A Bowl of Broth

7. He was a simple faithful creature, the sort that would have carried a snail half-a-mile to eat somebody else's plants sooner than put his foot on it.
Green Oranges

8. In general the worst thing you can do for anybody is to give them money, because in the first place it's easy-come, and in the second place instead of being grateful they think it mean of you not to give them more than you did.
Green Oranges

9. A man's happiness is in his wife's hands, anyway. If she's not actually with him she can always get at him.
Back to Ballygullion

10. We don't try to make jokes in Ulster. We say serious things in a way that makes them appear funny when you see how serious they are.
The Ballygullion Bus

Mick
Doyle

1. A gentle hand vibrated my body. I tried valiantly not to wake up but failed. My mind was responding in slow motion, running relentlessly through the familiar check list: testicles, spectacles, vallet and vatch.
Doyler

2. This particular Paddy confesses that it was frightening for him to realise that at the very moment both people said 'I do' he was transported from a snivelling, guilt-ridden self-conscious randy single man into a raving sex maniac with a game licence who was exhorted to procreate henceforth like bunnies in Ballybunnion.
Doyler

3. After we played Romania in Donnybrook in the 1980-81 season John Reason of the *Daily Telegraph* approached Willie Duggan and myself as we came off the pitch. Willie had just played one of the best games I'd seen him play for Leinster. John asked me for my observations on the game. I replied that we had decided to go out in the first half to soften them up and kick the proverbial shit out of them. Duggan drew deeply on his cigarette butt and through a halo of carcinogens fixed a beady eye on Reason and said: 'And it went so well for us, John, that we had a

quick word at half time and decided to kick the shit out of them in the second half!'
Doyler

Roddy
Doyle

4. Deco cupped his crotch in both hands (although one would have done) and roared: – 'I've a bugle here yeh can blow on, 'melda.'
The Commitments

5. That was the first time they'd done the business in a good while; two months nearly. Made love. He'd never called it that; it sounded thick. Riding your wife was more than just riding, especially when yis hadn't done it in months, but – he could never have said Let's make love to Veronica; she'd have burst out laughing at him.
The Van

6. I loved the smell off the bottle. I put hot water in it and emptied it and smelled it; I put my nose to the hole, nearly in it. Lovely. You didn't just fill it with water – my ma showed me; you had to lay the bottle on its side and slowly pour the water in or else air got trapped and the rubber rotted and burst. I jumped on Sinbad's bottle. Nothing happened. I didn't do it again. Sometimes when nothing happened it was really getting ready to happen.
Paddy Clarke Ha Ha Ha

1. I said one Hail Mary and four Our Fathers, because I preferred the Our Fathers to the Hail Mary and it was longer and better.
Paddy Clarke Ha Ha Ha

2. Daniel Boone was dressed in a green jacket with a white collar and stringy bits hanging off the sleeves. He had a fur hat with a red bobbin. He looked like one of the women in the cake shop in Raheny.
Paddy Clarke Ha Ha Ha

3. The ones at the back got the hardest spellings; instead of asking them, say eleven threes, he'd ask them eleven elevens or eleven twelves.
Paddy Clarke Ha Ha Ha

4. I was good at waiting for the scab to be ready. I never rushed. I waited until I was sure it was hollow, sure that the crust had lifted off my knee. It came off neat and tidy and there was no blood underneath, just a red mark; that was the knee being fixed. Scabs were made by things in your blood called corpuscles. There were thirty-five billion corpuscles in your blood. They made the scabs to stop you from bleeding to death.
Paddy Clarke Ha Ha Ha

5. It wasn't lots of little fights. It was one big one, rounds of the same fight. And it wouldn't stop after fifteen rounds like in boxing.

It was like one of the matches from the olden days where they wore no gloves and they kept punching till one of them was knocked out or killed. Ma and Da had gone way past Round Fifteen; they'd been fighting for years – it made sense now – but the breaks between the rounds were getting shorter, that was the big difference.
Paddy Clarke Ha Ha Ha

Charles
Dromgoole

6. He never liked to see a witness held up to ridicule; 'we laugh today and forget it tomorrow,' he would say; 'but the echoes of that laugh of ours will make that man's life a misery for months.'
in *The Old Munster Circuit* by Maurice Healy

Alan
Dukes

7. Yesterday's heroes have turned out not only to have feet of clay but to have no backbone at all.
The Irish Times, March 1993

8. [Of John Bruton] It's stimulating to talk to him because he is a ferment of new ideas, but if you are not in the business of wanting a ferment, then it can be a bit confusing.
The Irish Times, January 1993

Anne
Dunlop

1. When I was in primary school we had a drawing on the wall of Northern Ireland with blue surrounding it. I thought Northern Ireland was an island until I was twelve.
The Pineapple Tart

2. She and Sarah are amazing. They keep on and on at each other because they both want to get the last word in first.
A Soft Touch

Lee
Dunne

3. I was torn apart with kindness and nobody should ever get that out of touch. Kindness should never hurt anyone the way it did me that day.
Goodbye to the Hill

4. Kindness was a quality that I didn't know much about. It's not something that blossoms in a jungle like The Hill, where ignorance and superstition and violence and hatred fester in each other's arms like sores.
Goodbye to the Hill

5. 'Nobody's going to give you anything if you tell them the truth. Do you think I'd have done all those mots if I'd told them the truth? 'Course I wouldn't. I tell them I'm a poet or a writer or a painter, depending on the mood I'm in. I recite them a few lines of Shakespeare or Yeats, and then I tell them I wrote it. That's what I do.'
Goodbye to the Hill

6. Things were happening all the time on The Hill. Babies were being born to people who couldn't afford to keep themselves. Old people were dying, most of them in poverty and loneliness from which death could only be a welcome release. And all over the place governments were coming and going like snuff at a wake and people were saying that this would happen and that would happen now that the war was over.
Goodbye to the Hill

7. The taxi driver was asked in for a drink, and more power to his elbow he didn't say no. Dublin taximen are like that. If the work interferes with the drinking, stop the work.
Goodbye to the Hill

8. He had started to wonder why she hadn't married again, then stopping when he thought of her six kids. Beautiful she might be, and fine of form, but there weren't too many fellas about who wanted a ready-made family of six. To put six into a woman like her, fair enough, but to feed somebody else's?
Does your Mother?

1. He had been unsuccessful as an amateur boxer, but as a street and pub fighter he had enjoyed unqualified success.
Does your Mother?

2. Alice Keogh hit Lynch at that moment. She didn't have to think that he was off guard, that the left side of his face was sitting there like a melon on a shelf. It was a reflex action, the unconscious bloom of the seed of self-preservation, planted early in the compost heap of her life.
Does your Mother?

Paul
Durcan

3. I'm the Kilfenora teaboy
And I'm not so very young,
But though the land is going to
    pieces
I will not take up the gun;
I am happy making tea,
I make lots of it when I can,
And when I can't – I just make do;
And I do a small bit of
    sheepfarming on the side.
Teresa's Bar

4. And I'm not only a famous
    teaboy,
I'm a famous caveman too;
I paint pictures by the hundred
But you can't sell walls;
Although the people praise my
    pictures
As well as my turf-perfumed
    blend

They rarely fling a fiver in my
    face;
Oh don't we do an awful lot of
    dying on the side?
Teresa's Bar

5. Every child has a madman on
    their street:
The only trouble about *our*
    madman is that he's our
    father.
Jesus, Break His Fall

6. The perplexed defendants
    stand upright in the dock
While round about their spiked
    and barred forecastle,
Like corpses of mutinous sailors
    strewn about the deck
Of a ghost schooner becalmed in
    summer heat,
Recline solicitors in suits and
    barristers in wigs and gowns,
Snoring in their sleeves.
Jesus, Break His Fall

7. When she asked me to keep an
    eye on her things
I told her I'd be glad to keep an
    eye on her things.
While she breakdanced off to the
    ladies' loo
I concentrated on keeping an eye
    on her things.
What are you doing? a Security
    Guard growled,
His moustache gnawing at the
    beak of his peaked cap.
When I told him that a young
    woman whom I did not know
Had asked me to keep an eye on
    her things, he barked:
Instead of keeping an eye on the
    things

Of a young woman whom you do
not know,
Keep an eye on your own things.
The Berlin Wall Café

1. When I reported to him our
passion he asked me her name.
When I told him I did not know
her name
He said that was how it should
always be –
That it was better for a man and a
woman
Not to know one another's
names;
That it was better for a man and a
woman
Never to know one another's
names,
The thing in passion being
anonymity.
A Snail in my Prime

2. There were not many fields
In which you had hopes for me
But sport was one of them.
On my twenty-first birthday
I was elected to play
For Grangegorman Mental
Hospital
In an away game
Against Mullingar Mental
Hospital.
I was a patient
In B Wing.
Sport

Barney
Eastwood

3. Going into the King's Hall is
like going into the lion's den –

you go in like a lion and go out
like a lamb.
On the WBO Title Fight, April
1994

Maria
Edgeworth

4. 'Yes, everybody who comes
from Ireland *will* have a fine
estate when somebody dies,' said
her grace. 'But what have they at
present?'
The Absentee

5. 'Promises are dangerous things
to ask or to give,' said Grace. 'Men
and naughty children never make
promises, especially promises to
be good, without longing to break
them the next minute.'
The Absentee

6. Miss Juliana O'Leary pointed
out to his lordship's attention a
picture over the drawing-room
chimney-piece. 'Is not it a fine
piece, my lord?' said she, naming
the price Mrs Raffarty had lately
paid for it at an auction. 'It has a
right to be a fine piece, indeed;
for it cost a fine price!'
The Absentee

7. 'If I thought it worth my while
to make him like me, he must,
sooner or later. I delight in seeing
people begin with me as they do
with olives, making all manner of
horrid faces and silly
protestations that they will never
touch an olive again as long as

they live; but, after a little time, these very folk grow so desperately fond of olives that there is no dessert without them. Isabel child, you are in the sweet line – but sweets cloy. You never heard of anybody living on marmalade, did ye?'
The Absentee

1. 'You know, I know, as who does not that has seen the world, that though a pretty woman is a mighty pretty thing, yet she is confoundedly in one's way when anything else is to be seen, heard – or understood.'
The Absentee

2. 'It is shameful to laugh at these people, indeed, Lady Dashfort, in their own house – the hospitable people who are entertaining us.'
    'Entertaining us! True, and if we are entertained, how can we help laughing?'
The Absentee

St John
Ervine

3. Well, you're honest anyway. I can't say I feel proud, though, when a man tells me to my face that the only attraction I have is my money – and even that isn't mine: it's father's.
Anthony and Anna

4. One special thing which happens to every man who gets married. He loses all the friends he had when he was a bachelor.

Why? They belong to his adventurous life, and his wife distrusts them. She sets herself, very stealthily, to discourage them from coming to her house. She finds fault with them. She enlarges on their faults and fails to say anything about their good points.
Anthony and Anna

5. You've probably heard of him. He's the well-known profiteer. Made all his money during the war, so, of course, he's very rich. Do you know, darling, that man gave his services to the country without salary, and was richer when he left the Government than he was before he joined it.
Anthony and Anna

6. When he takes me out to lunch he gives me champagne! Champagne, my dear, in the afternoon! I always feel like a barmaid spending a week-end with a bookie!
Anthony and Anna

7. I told you, I live by my wits. When I speak the exact truth, nobody believes me, but if I were to tell you that I was the Governor of the Bank of England, you'd believe me at once.
Anthony and Anna

8. You're writing under false pretences, Mr Dunwoody. All the best authors have at least epilepsy, but you don't seem to have anything.
Anthony and Anna

1. Many women can write, and, alas, do; but how few women can be charming!
Anthony and Anna

2. It does us good to get into an effete atmosphere every once in a while. It helps us to go back and cope with America. The monotony of European diet is very soothing to the American stomach! . . .
Anthony and Anna

3. A waiter 'ardly ever sees people except when they're eating, and they don't look romantic then. There's times, miss, when the 'ole of humanity seems to me like a great big mouth, swallerin' things.
Anthony and Anna

4. You were a morbid child, an' you're a morbid woman. Nothin' contents you but to be thinkin' of hell's blazes. You can't enjoy a fire like any dacent, reasonable woman that's out for a bit of entertainment.
Boyd's Shop

5. You can't go up to a man nowadays, especially if you move in the same social circle, and say, 'Is it well with your soul?' or ask him if he's saved.
Boyd's Shop

6. One of the first things I'd do if I had Donaghrea would be a really tip-top Literary and Debating Society. Get all the leading authors of the day down to deliver a lecture. Even if they can't talk, people like to have a look at them.
Boyd's Shop

7. Well, everybody til their taste, of course, but the kind of minister I like is the one that, when he mentions hell, makes you feel as if you were in it.
Boyd's Shop

8. Imagine the state the world would be in if nobody drunk nothin'! Thousan's of distillery men on the dole. Guinness's Brewery bankrupt! Troops an' battalions of dacent publicans sellin' matches in the streets! My God, it's fearful to think of!
Boyd's Shop

9. In my experience, Adam, when you tamper with a system, no matter how slightly, you do harm that will spread until you have destroyed the entire system. Treat a bastard as if it were a legitimate child, and how long will that marriage last?
Friends and Relations

10. That's intellectual wit, I suppose. I don't think much of it. I've heard a lot of that sort of stuff from Arthur. It's all right in undergraduates, but not in adult men.
Friends and Relations

1. There's a man in the Bible I've often envied: Melchisidec, that had no relations of any shape or size. I'd like to resemble him, to be destitute of every kind of tie, no kindred, no home, no country, nothing that binds me to any mortal thing.
Friends and Relations

2. I'm what's called a critic's author. My reviews are good and my sales appalling. I have the largest following of people who don't read me of any author in the history of literature.
Friends and Relations

3. The fool of the family used to be in the Navy. Now he writes books.
Friends and Relations

4. Can't you say anything but 'why not'? Hundreds of pounds have been spent on your education, but you've got the most limited vocabulary of any man I know. Why not? Why not? Why not? This country's over-run by people that ask questions, but don't listen to answers.
Friends and Relations

5. Ah, drink's the curse of Ireland. It is, indeed. If it isn't whiskey, it's porter, and if it isn't porter, it's tea, an' sure, tea's the worst of the lot. The tea drunkards of Ireland, poor souls!
Friends and Relations

6. FANNY: He's hardly in his grave an hour yet!
ARTHUR: How long must he be in there before I can speak about him naturally?
Friends and Relations

George
Farquhar

7. The pride of these virtuous women is more insufferable than the immodesty of prostitutes.
The Constant Couple

8. An esteem grafted in old age is hardly rooted out, years stiffen their opinions with their bodies, and old zeal is only to be cozened by young hypocrisy.
The Constant Couple

9. To save his pretty face for the women he always turned his back upon the enemy. He was a man of honour – for the ladies.
The Constant Couple

10. I hate all those that don't love me, and slight all those who do. Would his whole deluding sex admire me, thus would I slight them all!
The Constant Couple

11. Of all the lovers I ever had, he was my greatest plague, for I could never make him uneasy.
The Constant Couple

1. Those that bear away the prize in the field, should boast the same success in the bedchamber.
The Constant Couple

2. Certainly most women magnify their modesty, for the same reason that cowards boast their courage, because they have least on't.
The Constant Couple

3. A gentleman! I tell you once more, Colonel, that I am a baronet, and have eight thousand pounds a year. I can dance, sing, ride, fence, understand the languages. Now I can't conceive how running you through the body should contribute one more jot to my gentility.
The Constant Couple

4. If your honour be concerned with a woman, get it out of her hands as soon as you can. An honourable lover is the greatest slave in nature; some will say, the greatest fool.
The Constant Couple

5. Drunkenness, Sir Harry, is the worst pretence a gentleman can make for rudeness: for the excuse is as scandalous as the fault.
The Constant Couple

6. Our comfort is, we have lived together, and shall die together; only with this difference, that I have lived like a fool, and shall die like a knave; and you have lived like a knave and shall die like a fool.
The Constant Couple

7. The travel of such fools as you doubly injures our country; you expose our native follies, which ridicules us among strangers; and return fraught only with their vices, which you vend here for fashionable gallantry. A travelling fool is as dangerous as a home-bred villain.
The Constant Couple

8. He gave me my portion, which was about fifteen hundred pound, and I have spent two thousand of it already.
The Twin Rivals

9. I have villainously murdered my fortune; and now its ghost, in the lank shape of Poverty, haunts me.
The Twin Rivals

10. When knaves of our sex, and fools of yours meet, they make the best jest in the world.
The Twin Rivals

11. I had rather, Mr Subtleman, it were his by justice and mine by law; for I would have strongest title.
The Twin Rivals

12. I knew a gentleman, three days buried, taken out of his grave, and his dead hand set to his last will (unless somebody made him sign another afterwards).
The Twin Rivals

1. I have a graceless son, a fellow that drinks and swears eternally, keeps a whore in every corner of the town: in short, he's fit for no kind of thing but a soldier.
The Twin Rivals

2. Show me that proud stoic that can bear success and champagne! Philosophy can support us in hard fortune, but who can have patience in prosperity?
The Twin Rivals

3. But for a woman! 'Sdeath, I have been constant to fifteen at a time, but never melancholy for one.
The Recruiting Officer

4. What, no bastards! And so many recruiting officers in town; I thought 'twas a maxim among them to leave as many recruits in the country as they carried out.
The Recruiting Officer

5. Silvia and I had once agreed to go to bed together, could we have adjusted preliminaries; but she would have the wedding before consummation, and I was for consummation before the wedding.
The Recruiting Officer

6. I'm resolved never to bind myself to a woman in my whole life, till I know whether I shall like her company for half an hour.
The Recruiting Officer

7. He has the most universal acquaintance of any man living, for he won't be alone, and nobody will keep him company twice.
The Recruiting Officer

8. The devil take all officers, I say; they do the nation more harm by debauching us at home, than they do good by defending us abroad.
The Recruiting Officer

9. One may like the love and despise the lover, I hope; as one may love the treason, and hate the traitor.
The Recruiting Officer

10. Things past, madam, can hardly be reckoned surprising, because we know them already.
The Recruiting Officer

11. You are no logician if you pretend to draw consequences from the actions of fools. There's no arguing by the rule of reason upon a science without principles, and such is their conduct; whim, unaccountable whim, hurries 'em on, like a man drunk with brandy before ten o'clock in the morning.
The Recruiting Officer

12. The devil is a very modest person, he seeks nobody unless they seek him first.
The Recruiting Officer

1. He means marriage, I think – but that, you know, is so odd a thing, that hardly any two people under the sun agree in the ceremony; some make it a sacrament, others a convenience, and others make it a jest.
The Recruiting Officer

2. I believe they talked of me, for they laughed consumedly.
The Beaux' Strategem

3. She has cured more people in and about Lichfield within ten years than the doctors have killed in twenty; and that's a bold word.
The Beaux' Strategem

4. We can't say that we have spent our fortunes, but that we have enjoyed 'em.
The Beaux' Strategem

5. If ever you marry, beware of a sullen, silent sot, one that's always musing, but never thinks. There's more diversion in a talking blockhead; and since a woman must wear chains, I would have the pleasure of hearing 'em rattle a little.
The Beaux' Strategem

6. First, it must be a plot, because there's a woman in't: secondly, it must be a plot, because there's a priest in't: thirdly, it must be a plot because there's French gold in't: fourthly, it must be a plot,

because I don't know what to make on't.
The Beaux' Strategem

7. Unless you have pity upon me, and smoke one pipe with me, I must e'en go home to my wife, and I'd rather go to the devil by half.
The Beaux' Strategem

8. The very timorous stag will kill in rutting time.
The Beaux' Strategem

Brian Faulkner

9. . . . it is not the truth which matters in Northern Ireland, but what people believe to be the truth.
The Irish Times, 1972

David Feherty

10. It was quite good fun watching John [Daly] dislodge a cubic yard of Kent every time he hit the ball. Even his divots were travelling farther than my shots.
The Irish Times, June 1993

11. He [Colin Montgomerie] looked like a bulldog licking piss off a nettle.
The Irish Times, June 1993

Laurence
Flanagan

1. In 1987 I enjoyed the privilege of lecturing to the Society of Antiquaries of Scotland. I prefaced my lecture with the remark that when I'd mentioned to some people at home in Belfast that I was to lecture to the SAS I got some funny looks. After the lecture one member of the audience came up and remarked that he was shattered that apart from himself nobody in the audience appeared to have understood.
Personal communication

Oliver J.
Flanagan

2. Let us hope and trust that there are sufficient proud and ignorant people left in this country to stand up to the intellectuals who are out to destroy faith and fatherland.
The Irish Times, 10 April 1971

3. There was no sex in Ireland before television.
Attrib.

Dónal
Foley

4. 'NUFF SAID
The Fianna Fail 'Silence on the North' campaign was launched at the weekend with a Monster Meeting in O'Connell Street. There were fifty bands, 500 cumainn present. The Taoiseach's appeal for silence was greeted with a roar of approval by 50,000 throats. Too much had been said about the Six Counties: the North now deserved our silence.
The Best of 'Man Bites Dog', reprinted from *The Irish Times*

5. The news of the administrative mistake made about the dole for single men has brought to light some further startling official errors. It emerged yesterday in Government circles that Article 44 of the Constitution – that is, the special place of the Catholic Church – was in fact a clerical error.
The Best of 'Man Bites Dog', reprinted from *The Irish Times*

6. THE WORD STEALERS
The National Union of Journalists and the gardai are co-operating in a drive to stop the crime of breaking into journalism. 'In recent years breaking into journalism has been on the increase at an alarming rate. Journalism is not a safe profession any more,' said the National Organiser of the NUJ The garda spokeman said that amateur thieves were largely involved in breaking into journalism, but too often they went on to bigger and better things like stealing headlines, grabbing by-lines, taking photographs. 'Later on they often

end up making headlines,' he
added grimly.
The Best of 'Man Bites Dog',
reprinted from *The Irish Times*

Percy
French

1. There are people who say
It is wrong to be gay
In this workaday world of ours;
They live far apart
From the pleasures of art
Discarding the sweets for the
    sours.
People I don't want to meet

2. Father's lost all the money he
    made.
I think it's the best bit of fun;
He says I must go into a trade
And make bricks like my
    gran'papa done.
Things that matter

3. We've not seen a doctor for
    weeks;
Pa looks like a Bowery Tough;
And Ma has got red in her cheeks
That isn't put on with a puff.
Things that matter

4. I want to find some place on
    earth
Where motors are unknown,
Where hydroplane ne'er skims
    the main,
Nor aeroplane's been flown.
A Reaction

5. 'Tis wisdom's golden rule
I do teach her till I tire
That every girl's a fool,
And every man a liar.
Whistlin' Phil McHugh

6. Oh! Joan, when first you saw
    the light you caused us much
    annoy,
For both your parents thought
    you might as well have been a
    boy.
*Lines written in Praise of Joan
Phyllis French*

7. Dear Lord – Aunt Jane is good
    I know
But then her smiles are scanty,
I do want to be good – but oh!
Not quite as good as Aunty.
A Little Girl's Prayer

8. When the cat has finished
    breakfast,
And is sitting by the fire,
The cat that all the tabby cats
Persistently admire,
When that most unpleasant
    animal
The dog, is out of doors,
And pussy thinks of how last
    night
He settled some old scores,
When he thinks about the big
    black cat
He knocked right off the tiles –
                                    He smiles.
Smiles

9. I have just come back from a
children's party. I am one of the
survivors. There are not many of
us.
*The Story of the Lion that
wouldn't eat Parsley*

1. When an artist goes to sketch in the West of Ireland, there is often trouble in getting a suitable place to stay. There are lodgings that advertise bed and board for five shillings, but you can't tell very often which is the bed and which is the board.
My Friend Finnegan

Brian
Friel

2. The details of the bird's possible loss interested him. 'Would he even have made the length of Limerick?' he asked the Fusilier.
    'At the very outside,' said the Fusilier.
    'If the north-Cork hawks didn't get him first.'
    'Bad brutes, them.'
    'They've been known to attack children – even north-Cork children.'
The Diviner

3. She was not greedy, Min, but she had a powerful regard for money – I suppose because we never had any.
The Diviner

4. TIM: For God's sake, I'm not even sure that I like Susan!
JACK: Who mentioned liking her, professor? You're going with her – that's all. And it's a perfect match: you're ugly and penniless, she's pretty and rich.
The Communication Cord

5. Two such wonderful phrases – 'I understand perfectly' and 'That is a lie' – a précis of life, aren't they?
The Communication Cord

6. PRINCESS: My brother, Josef, had the first accordion ever brought into Russia. My father lit a bonfire in the yard and burned the damn thing before the whole houshold. Then he whipped Josef with his own hunting crop until he apologised publicly to everybody – family and servants. Ha-ha. That ended damned accordions in our house!
Fathers and Sons

7. MAIRE: We should all be learning to speak English. That's what Dan O'Connell said last month in Ennis. He said the sooner we all learn to speak English the better.
DOALTY: It's Irish he uses when he's travelling around scrounging votes.
BRIDGET: And sleeping with married women. Sure no woman's safe from that fella.
Translations

8. HUGH: Who is she talking about?
MAIRE: I'm talking about Daniel O'Connell.
HUGH: Does she mean that little Kerry politician?
Translations

1. MANUS: What's 'incorrect' about the place-names we have here?
OWEN: Nothing at all. They're just going to be standardised.
MANUS: You mean changed into English?
OWEN: Where there's ambiguity, they'll be Anglicised.
Translations

2. OWEN: Back to first principles. What are we trying to do?
YOLLAND: Good question.
OWEN: We are trying to denominate and at the same time describe that tiny area of soggy, rocky, sandy ground where that little stream enters the sea, an area known locally as Bun na hAbhann. . . Burnfoot! What about Burnfoot?
YOLLAND: Good, Roland, Burnfoot's good.
Translations

James
Galway

3. Some of the Lodges were very Protestant, with the philosophy, 'Don't enjoy yourself – otherwise you won't get into heaven'.
An Autobiography

4. The subscription to the band was a tanner a week but they weren't always too particular about collecting the money and I think I still owe them about twenty quid.
An Autobiography

5. Belfast used to more or less shut down on a Sunday. A lot of people like that sort of atmosphere; others take the view that morgues are for dead people.
An Autobiography

6. It never occurred to me, or anybody else living in Carnalea Street, that we were underprivileged. We were too busy getting what fun we could out of life to worry about that sort of thing.
An Autobiography

7. Like most Belfast Protestants, I accepted every word of the Bible as literally true. I never stopped to think that the Book might not even have been written originally in English.
An Autobiography

8. People imagine that Galway is a typical Irish name but, in fact, it is pretty rare and I like to point out that there are only about a half-dozen Galways in the Irish telephone book – and one of those is a Bishop.
An Autobiography

Bob
Geldof

9. We had difficulty getting good enough security to satisfy insurers. Most of the security men in Dublin were so well known and so violent that their very presence instigated trouble.
Is That It?

1. I knew he was Special Branch because of his sheepskin coat.
Is That It?

2. It was like my life generally. Like a swan it would be all serenity on top but paddling like fuck underneath.
Is That It?

3. The boy who showed me how to masturbate saw God while on drugs and then became a monk.
Is That It?

4. Sex was a competitive event in those days and the only thing you could take as a certainty was that everyone else was lying, just as you were.
Is That It?

Oliver St John
Gogarty

---

5. He [Yeats] won the Nobel Prize for Poetry in the face of the competition of the civilised world. The Corporation of Dublin gave the Freedom of the City to a man who won the Derby with a horse.
Going Native

6. The visitor may enjoy going to Ireland but no native enjoys being in it all the time. Ireland is the last place for an Irishman to thrive.
Going Native

7. The English for centuries have been in the habit of coming over here and becoming more Irish than the Irish themselves. It is high time that one of us returned the compliment.
Going Native

8. 'What shall it profit a man, if he shall gain the whole world, and lose his own soul?' That must be why the English gained the whole world.
Going Native

9. England has forgiven us magnanimously for all the injuries she inflicted on us long ago.
Going Native

10. The Irish take friendship for granted; they think that there is time enough to show their affection.
Going Native

11. The Welsh language is very useful in Wales. It persuades the English tourist that he is in a foreign country without leaving his own. Those wonderful words made without vowels, like pastry without eggs . . .
Going Native

12. There are no cataracts on the Thames. It is something like the river Shannon, which has hardly enough energy to take itself out of the country.
Going Native

1. It is understood that every one in England has made sacrifices for his country whether in this century or the last half-dozen centuries. That is what makes it such a pleasant place in which to live: they have got over their self-sacrifice and all that sort of thing is out of the way and now they are making up with all their might, as it were, for days of discipline.
Going Native

2. From both a social and a military point of view, Englishmen have it on all the world. They are enjoying the present because their descendants may have to sacrifice somebody or other in the future.
Going Native

3. How wonderfully a platitude can be used to convey a faintly sinister significance in England.
Going Native

4. 'If you were in the middle of an orgasm, would you like to be spoken to?'
Going Native

5. The doctor was a diplomatic and intelligent man. Only for this latter qualification he might have had a very distinguished career in the Foreign Office.
Going Native

6. Normality is the enemy of distinction.
Going Native

7. He specialised in his patients. In this way he was a real specialist, in contradistinction to the town specialists who are identified with certain diseases or disasters to such an extent that it is as much as your reputation is worth to be seen on their doorsteps.
Going Native

8. There is something very lascivious about the minor notes of an organ when played in a fashion corresponding to strip-tease.
Going Native

9. Dancing always seems to me to be superfluous: I am ridiculous enough without it.
Going Native

10. What she wanted was an echo, not an ear.
Going Native

11. I have a watch with only one hand (to prevent my being reduced to keeping appointments).
Going Native

12. Unfortunately the worst imputations are the improvable. If they cannot be proved, they cannot be repudiated.
Going Native

13. I wondered who it was told me that the English were not dreamers, poets and sentimentalists; and who the devil told me that we Irish were? I do

not mind being fooled about others, but to be fooled about myself wakens my resentment.
Going Native

1. What you take for lying in an Irishman is only his attempt to put an herbaceous border on stark reality.
Going Native

2. Whenever I see a dog, I see in it a prevented family. The dog is the wagging symbol of birth control, of the sex sublimation of the race.
Going Native

3. I am well aware that when a patient begins to think that his doctor does not understand him he begins to be incurable.
Going Native

4. Treachery is, even before humbug, the one thing I detest. A traitor to one's friends. That is to my mind far worse than being a traitor to one's country or rather that set of vested interests, the gangs we call governments nowadays.
Going Native

5. When an Englishman gets his teeth into what he thinks is a joke (it has to be a pun of some obvious form), it is useless to argue with him until he has recovered from his lock-jaw. He simply cannot take anything seriously for an hour. It is best to retire and catch him again on another wave when he has forgotten his own wit.
Going Native

6. The names in this book are real, the characters fictitious.
As I was going down Sackville Street

7. I will ask him a question which I wish to have resolved, for he is the brainiest fellow in Dublin, an honest man, and what is more, an honest solicitor.
As I was going down Sackville Street

8. 'It is trying work, conducting a National Library,' he said. 'You can have no idea of the difficulties which confront me. I am worn to a shadow, as one might say, endeavouring to keep the peace. I am at the disposal, at the mercy of a public, some of whom are not trained for a room, not to speak of a library.'
As I was going down Sackville Street

9. He introduced jazz into English verse, on account of his mixed blood no doubt. There is black blood in him somewhere, that is why he was called Browning.
As I was going down Sackville Street

10. Politics is the chloroform of the Irish people, or, rather, the hashish.
As I was going down Sackville Street

1. There is nothing more sinister than the humility of the mean.
As I was going down Sackville Street

2. A little slogan formed itself in my mind, a cry to the women of Ireland: 'More petting, less politics.'
As I was going down Sackville Street

3. Nobody can betray Ireland: it does not give him the chance; it betrays him first.
As I was going down Sackville Street

4. The money spent in attempting to turn this nation into a race of bilingualists ignorant and gullible in two languages, would have given Dublin spacious streets and boulevards and restored it to the place it held as the Seventh City of Christendom before Napoleonic Paris was built.
As I was going down Sackville Street

5. Dublin has one advantage: it is easy to get out of it.
As I was going down Sackville Street

6. The Government here has freedom from the Press. This is compensated for by the fact that it owns a Press which has no freedom from the Government . . .
As I was going down Sackville Street

7. That is one of Dublin's famous inventions – soda. It was invented in Sackville Street. The well is under Nelson's Pillar. It is a temperance drink, but it is fated to be associated with whiskey until the end of time. A perfect proof that not only is there a Providence, but Providence disapproves of teetotallers.
As I was going down Sackville Street

8. It is strange how much it takes to make me drunk in boring company; I can get drunk without a glass with my good companions.
As I was going down Sackville Street

9. Can it be that because none of them is truly bawdy, none is truly great? Can it be that the further men remove themselves or are removed from the opposite sex the further they are removed from the service of humanity?
As I was going down Sackville Street

10. When we were walking past the Bailey it reminded her that we were twenty-three years married today! 'What do you propose?' she asked. 'Three minutes' silence,' said I.
As I was going down Sackville Street

11. I do not think that you are right in calling the President a Dago. He is no more a Dago than Deputy Nugget. A Dago is a

citizen of San Diego, and one who would certainly think it an impertinence if you called him an Irishman or held him responsible for the present mess. He is more Irish perhaps than any of us, seeing that he looks like something uncoiled from the Book of Kells.
As I was going down Sackville Street

1. You have ruined all the graffiti. You can't find anything in a piss-house now but political remarks. It's always a sign of decline in the fortunes of a country.
As I was going down Sackville Street

2. I should hate to have my pubs stalked by German professors who took pub-crawling seriously. The moment our pubs become the subject of literature, that is the moment they are undone. Even we who patronise them would become self-conscious. The last thing drink should do is to make one self-conscious.
As I was going down Sackville Street

3. When it comes to governing under democratic conditions you have either to reduce the people to your own level of mediocrity or reduce yourself to theirs. As a rule it is a compromise which brings both to a lower level than either held.
As I was going down Sackville Street

4. Why does every educated Irishman regret that he is Irish? Is it the education, the country or himself that is wrong? Or is it wrong to be educated? Or is it wrong to regret?
As I was going down Sackville Street

5. If any signs of inferiority were manifested they were due to artificial and arbitary rules, British in origin, which sought to lay down laws even for eating asparagus. The asparagus, to give it its due, revolted and refused to be hung up by the green end.
As I was going down Sackville Street

6. I told him how Bernard Shaw went to church the other day and, when they passed him the plate, moved aside murmuring 'Press'.
As I was going down Sackville Street

7. 'But I have never done the people any harm.'
   'That's just it. You see, I have been in many uncivilised places where human life was of little consequence. I have met savages of every description. And the worst position you can place yourself in with them is to do them no harm.'
As I was going down Sackville Street

1. . . . and that shows that a thing may be a universally accepted fact, and yet be true.
As I was going down Sackville Street

2. I only went to Oxford because I was not clever enough for Trinity, Dublin, as Mahaffy said of Oscar Wilde.
As I was going down Sackville Street

3. London with its law and order sometimes chokes me. There are three or four people too many in it. It takes an hour to drive to the edge of it, and then I find that the countryside is almost as much built on.
As I was going down Sackville Street

4. Ireland is a place or state of repose where souls suffer from the hope that the time will come when they may go abroad.
As I was going down Sackville Street

5. It is not in falling between two stools that the tragedy consists, but in falling off each stool in turn.
As I was going down Sackville Street

6. Did you not hear that the Lord punished him by substituting *angina pectoris* for his pectoral cross?
As I was going down Sackville Street

7. Some people like to show their catholicism by entertaining the narrow-minded.
As I was going down Sackville Street

8. Parsons hate laymen to take their words out of their mouths.
As I was going down Sackville Street

9. That's this country all over! Not content with a contradiction in terms, it must go on to an antithesis in ideas. 'Temperance Hotel'! You might as well speak of a celibate kip!
As I was going down Sackville Street

10. The worst thought of all is that the sweet odour of the new-mown grass depends on cumarin, a chemical, of course. Why can't chemists keep their hands off the scent of new-mown hay?
Tumbling in the Hay

11. He left TCD after a long and successful career as a Scotsman.
Tumbling in the Hay

12. My aunt, of course, says that nobody can afford to drink at all; which is absurd, for it is obvious that in a little time nobody could afford to sell drink to insolvents.
Tumbling in the Hay

13. 'Will you bring that lobster, quick?' some host of Oscar Wilde said to the waiter. 'May I have mine dead?' Oscar tentatively enquired.
Tumbling in the Hay

1. I wasn't much good at self-sacrifice. There was no need to be. So many people were sacrificing me at the moment that it would have seemed superfluous to try it on myself.
Tumbling in the Hay

2. I wasn't cocksure, for I knew the sportsmen in the North, and I was still lumpy where I had got kicked by a sporting spectator as I was backing over the sideline to take a corner against Cliftonville last winter.
Tumbling in the Hay

3. Portadown is regarded unfavourably by some, who would let their prejudice take them so far as to appeal to others to withold at its station certain hygienic amenities recommended by the railway company. This prejudice has even found vent in writing – anonymous, I must confess. Somebody had scrawled under the official notice in the carriage, 'You are requested not to use the lavatory when the train is standing at a station,' the words 'except at Portadown'.
Tumbling in the Hay

4. You might as well try to employ a boa constrictor as a tape-measure as to go to a lawyer for legal advice.
Tumbling in the Hay

5. 'I took her aside and confided to her my little trouble about the flatulance. "It's only wind," sez she. Think of her audacity! "It's only wind," sez she to me. "Only wind? Only wind?" sez I. "Have ye never heard of the Tay Bridge disaster?"'
Tumbling in the Hay

6. Where did I put *The Irish Times* – the paper that puts the births before the marriages?
Tumbling in the Hay

7. 'I'd rather be a whore any day of the week than one of those barristers. A whore sells her body; but a barrister sells his bloody mind to the highest bidder. A whore can call her soul her own.'
Tumbling in the Hay

8. There is a lot of rot talked about the effect of vice on the countenance. It gives some faces, if anything, a liberal look, but it largely depends on the kind of vice. Avarice was written by Nature's hieroglyphic on the face of Mrs Mack.
Tumbling in the Hay

9. 'If I took nothing but pints, I'd be full before I was half drunk; and if I took nothing but small whiskies, I'd be drunk before I was full.'
Tumbling in the Hay

10. The Irish have wit but little humour. They cannot laugh at the battle while they are involved in the broil of life.
Tumbling in the Hay

1. One friend of Gogarty's had a glass eye, and one evening at dinner at Jammet's, Oliver, at the end of the dinner, lifted his glass and said, 'Drink to me with thine only eye.'
in *Irish Literary Portraits* by W. R. Rodgers

2. [de Valera] is the Spanish onion in the Irish stew.
Attrib.

3. [of Frank O'Connor] A country boy with hair in his nose and hair in his ears and a briefcase in his hand.
in *My Father's Son* by Frank O'Connor

4. An Irishman is someone who wishes he was somewhere else.
Attrib.

5. [In a New York bar in the 1950s, trying to tell an anecdote over the noise of a jukebox] 'Oh, dear God in heaven, that I should find myself thousands of miles from home, an old man at the mercy of every retarded son of a bitch who has a nickel to drop in that bloody illuminated coal scuttle.'
Attrib.

6. I'm the queerest young fellow
   of whom you've ever heard
My mother's a Jew and my
   father's a bird.
With Joseph the joiner I cannot
   agree
So here's to disciples and Calvary.

If anyone says that I amn't divine
He'll get no free drinks when I
   hand round the wine
But have to drink water and wish
   it were plain
That I make when the wine
   becomes water again.

Goodbye now goodbye! Write
   down all I said
And tell Tom, Dick and Harry I
   rose from the dead.
What's bred in the bone cannot
   fail me to fly
And Oliver's breezy. Goodbye,
   now, goodbye.
from *The Ballad of Joking Jesus*

Oliver
Goldsmith

7. At a dinner so various, at such
   a repast,
Who'd not be a glutton, and stick
   to the last?
Here, waiter! more wine, let me
   sit while I'm able,
Till all my companions sink
   under the table.
Retaliation

8. The scourge of impostors, the
   terror of quacks;
Come all ye quack bards, and ye
   quacking divines,
Come and dance on the spot
   where your tyrant reclines;
When Satire and Censure
   encircl'd his throne,
I fear'd for your safety, I fear'd for
   my own.
Retaliation

1. He cast off his friends, as a
    huntsman his pack,
For he knew when he pleas'd he
    could whistle them back.
Retaliation

2. That a Scot may have humour,
    I had almost said wit:
This debt to thy mem'ry I cannot
    refuse,
Thou best humour'd man with
    the worst humour'd muse.
Retaliation

3. Here lies David Garrick –
    describe me, who can,
An abridgement of all that was
    pleasant in man.
As an actor, confess'd without
    rival to shine;
As a wit, if not first, in the very
    first line.
Retaliation

4. Our Garrick's a salad; for in
    him we see
Oil, vinegar, sugar, and saltiness
    agree.
Retaliation

5. Though equal to all things, for
    all things unfit;
Too nice for a statesman, too
    proud for a wit.
Retaliation

6. I'll give thee something yet
    unpaid,
Not less sincere than civil:
I'll give thee – Ah! too charming
    maid,
I'll give thee – to the Devil.
The Gift

7. Logicians have but ill defin'd
As rational the human kind;
Reason, they say, belongs to man,
But let them prove it if they can.
The Logicians Refuted

8. Who ever knew an honest brute
At law his neighbour prosecute,
Bring action for assault and
    battery,
Or friends beguile with lies and
    flattery?
The Logicians Refuted

9. Brutes never meet in bloody
    fray,
Nor cut each other's throats, for
    pay.
The Logicians Refuted

10. Of beasts, it is confessed, the
    ape
Comes nearest us in human
    shape;
Like man he imitates each
    fashion,
And malice is his ruling passion;
But both in malice and grimaces
A courtier any ape surpasses.
The Logicians Refuted

11. She strove the neighbourhood
    to please,
With manners wond'rous
    winning,
And never followed wicked
    ways, –
Unless when she was sinning.
*An Elegy on that Glory of
her Sex*

1. At church, in silks and satins
   new,
With hoops of monstrous size,
She never slumber'd in her pew, –
But when she shut her eyes.
*An Elegy on that Glory of
her Sex*

2. Skill'd in no other arts was
   she,
But dressing, patching, repartee;
And, just as humour rose or fell,
By turns a slattern or a belle;
'Tis true she dress'd with modern
   grace,
Half naked at a ball or race;
But when at home, at board or
   bed,
Five greasy nightcaps wrapp'd her
   head.
The Double Transformation

3. The wound it seem'd both sore
   and sad
To every Christian eye;
And while they swore the dog was
   mad,
They swore the man would die.

But soon a wonder came to light,
That show'd the rogues they lied:
The man recover'd of the bite,
The dog it was that died.
Elegy on the Death of a Mad Dog

4. Here lies poor Ned Purdon,
   from misery freed,
Who long was a bookseller's hack;
He led such a damnable life in
   this world, –
I don't think he'll wish to come
   back.
Epitaph on Edward Purdon

5. Your mandate I got,
You may all go to pot;
Had your senses been right,
You'd have sent before night;
As I hope to be saved,
I put off being shaved;
For I could not make bold,
While the matter was cold,
To meddle in suds,
Or to put on my duds.
*Verses in Reply to an Invitation
to Dinner*

6. SIR WILLIAM HONEYWOOD: My
letters to him during my
employment in Italy, taught him
only that philosophy which might
prevent, not defend his errors.
JARVIS: Faith, begging your
honour's pardon, I'm sorry they
taught him any philosophy at all;
it has only served to spoil him.
This same philosophy is a good
horse in the stable, but an arrant
jade on a journey.
The Good-Natur'd Man

7. His good nature arises rather
from his fears of offending the
importunate, than his desire of
making the deserving happy.
The Good-Natur'd Man

8. It's the way with them all, from
the scullion to the privy-
counsellor. If they have a bad
master, they keep quarrelling
with him; if they have a good
master, they keep quarrelling
with one another.
The Good-Natur'd Man

1. His very mirth is an antidote to all gaiety, and his appearance has a stronger effect on my spirits than an undertaker's shop.
The Good-Natur'd Man

2. Friendship is a disinterested commerce between equals; love, an abject intercourse between tyrants and slaves.
The Good-Natur'd Man

3. Every age has its admirers, ladies. While you, perhaps, are trading among the warmer climates of youth, there ought to be some to carry on a useful commerce in the frozen latitudes beyond fifty.
The Good-Natur'd Man

4. Poetry is a pretty thing enough for our wives and daughter; but not for us.
The Good-Natur'd Man

5. MISS RICHLAND: You danced that night with the most awkward woman in company, because you saw nobody else would take her out.
HONEYWOOD: Yes; and was rewarded the next night, by dancing with the finest woman in company, whom everybody wished to take out.
The Good-Natur'd Man

6. You may be a Darby, but I'll be no Joan, I promise you.
She Stoops to Conquer

7. A reserved lover, it is said, always makes a suspicious husband.
She Stoops to Conquer

8. When Methodist preachers come down,
A-preaching that drinking is sinful,
I'll wager the rascals a crown,
They always preach best with a skinful.
She Stoops to Conquer

9. If you know neither the road you are going, nor where you are, nor the road you came, the first thing I have to inform you is, that – you have lost your way.
She Stoops to Conquer

10. Travellers, George, must pay in all places. The only difference is, that in good inns, you pay dearly for luxuries; in bad inns, you are fleeced and starved.
She Stoops to Conquer

11. An impudent fellow may counterfeit modesty, but I'll be hanged if a modest man can ever counterfeit impudence.
She Stoops to Conquer

12. Happy man! You have talents and art to captivate any woman. I'm doomed to adore the sex, and yet to converse with the only part of it I despise.
She Stoops to Conquer

1. An honest man may rob himself of his own at any time.
She Stoops to Conquer

2. O! sir, I must not tell my age. They say women and music should never be dated.
She Stoops to Conquer

3. The chest contriv'd a double
   debt to pay,
A bed by night, a chest of drawers
   by day.
The Deserted Village

Sir Tyrone
Guthrie

4. Edward can't dance. My dear, if we polish the floor Edward will simply roll about like a porpoise in the sea.
The Flowers are not for You to Pick

5. And those awful people from Annagh-ma-Kerrig.
The Flowers are not for You to Pick

6. An absolutely empty mind waiting like an empty room to be furnished, or like snow without footmarks. And the first impression your baby will get, instead of being pure and noble and lovely will be that awful wallpaper in Rose's bedroom and that ugly old beast of a nurse with a wart on her chin.
Squirrel's Cage

7. Radio Éireann occupies two frowsty floors high, high above Dublin's General Post Office. You enter by a sort of tradesman's entrance in a side street. Discouraged elderly attendants tell you that the lift is out of order, so you toil up endless stairs which smell of the lavatories and of mutton fat from the Post Office Canteen.
A Life in the Theatre

8. It always seems odd that for Irish Protestants the cross is not a Christian symbol, nor a symbol of love; it is a detested and specifically Roman Catholic sign.
A Life in the Theatre

9. If you want to be nicely received in Belfast or Portadown, carry a crescent, carry a hammer and sickle; wear if you will, a scarlet letter or a green carnation. People will still be their wonted, wholesome civil selves. If, however, you want to be beaten, reviled and possibly stoned to death, display prominently that emblem which proclaims that the Son of Man died to save sinners.
A Life in the Theatre

10. Belfast was a salutary shock. To begin with it looked so different from any of the other places where I had lived. Here are no dreaming spires, no grey old colleges. Nature has been kind;

the city stands on the estuary of the River Lagan, with soft green hills to the south and south-east; the sea to the east; and to the north, mountains . . . Man's work is vile. The river is a polluted conglomeration of shipyards, gasworks, coal basins; into it pours the refuse of the great mills, which send linen and rope to the far corners of the earth.
A Life in the Theatre

1. With the possible exceptions of Jersualem and Mecca, Belfast must be the most religion-conscious city in the world.
A Life in the Theatre

2. The very public conveniences are inscribed not with the sort of messages which you find in the conveniences of other cities, but with 'God Sees You', 'Christ died for sinners', 'To Hell with the Pope', 'Up Sinn Fein' and most frequent of all, that eerie query: 'Eternity Where?'
A Life in the Theatre

Charles J. Haughey

3. Who writes *The Irish Times* editorials, anyway? They read like they have been done by an old woman sitting in a bath with the water getting cold around her fanny!
in *Charlie* by T. Ryle Dwyer

Dermot Healy

4. In a small hostelry, up the dishevelled stairs among loud demurring students who flaunted an adopted Gaelic and what little knowledge of alcoholism they had, she drank pints of Guinness in the early flamboyant style of a girl celebrating new values and wisdom, eager for a person to steal a promise from the ennui of the drinkers.
Banished Misfortune

5. It took a while for McFarland to see confirmed in him and among the others a sense of other realities than being Irish; drink should let the mind wander to the present even foregoing the recent if not altogether past.
Banished Misfortune

6. 'You can learn to live with anyone,' Saul had said, 'it's imperial to me.'
Banished Misfortune

7. They both hit the water like baby elephants, with great splashes and roars. The water level rises.
    Pat Whelan gets out to jump in again.
    He doesn't seem to mind that his drawers have fallen a little, so that his hairy arse is showing and

when he turns around we can see his mickey, all shrivelled up with the water, like something made out of putty and not finished.
Banished Misfortune

Maurice
Healy

1. The only deviations from accuracy that have been intentional are such as had already given perspective to the facts when they were told to or by me on circuit. By this I mean that a Corkman likes to tell a story as it should be told; the garb may be elaborated, but the body is not deformed.
The Old Munster Circuit

2. The Irish could never understand why the severity should all be directed against one side, when the root evil was all on the other.
The Old Munster Circuit

3. I think that all County Courts in Ireland were built from a single plan in the Office of the Board of Works. Some were smaller and some larger than others; but they reproduced the same discomfort in every country town.
The Old Munster Circuit

4. The Englishman goes into a court of law unwillingly, fearfully, and especially apprehensive of cross-examination. No doubt there are occasional witnesses of that kind in Ireland, too; but the vast majority go to give their evidence as a cricketer walks to the wicket. Each is confident he will not be bowled until he has knocked up a good score; each is very disappointed if the bowler limits his efforts to preventing the score from rising, and does not attack his wicket.
The Old Munster Circuit

5. 'Tell me, in your country what happens to a witness who does not tell the truth?' 'Begor, me Lord,' replies the Irishman, with a candour that disarmed all criticism, 'I think his side usually wins!'
The Old Munster Circuit

6. Kerry and Cork have always produced the best brains in Ireland (need I stress the point that I reckon myself a Corkman?)
The Old Munster Circuit

7. A learned old schoolmaster in Cork was once described to me as a man who could spit in nine languages.
The Old Munster Circuit

8. Father and son used to wander from town to town in a funny little car, trespass upon which Girvin prevented by always bringing the gear-lever into the bar-room with him, where one or other of us would affect to

mistake it for the poker, and be only just prevented from poking the fire with it.
The Old Munster Circuit

1. All of our candidates had been wiped out except Tom himself, who told the House that there were two united Irish parties, of which he was one.
The Old Munster Circuit

2. Standish [O'Grady] was, I think, the fattest man I have ever seen; an aunt of mine once gazed at him in amazement and murmured in awestruck tones: 'To think that's all one man!'
The Old Munster Circuit

3. Some of those who had been the most eager of Sir Edward Carson's gallopers showed a strange lack of enthusiasm when the chance of fighting became real.
The Old Munster Circuit

Timothy Healy

4. [When a young forester, giving evidence for the plaintiff admitted he was only twenty-two and had been a forester for only two years] 'A regular babe in the wood, my Lord.'
in *Timothy Healy: Memories and Anecdotes* by Sir Dunbar Plunket Barton

5. [When a judge complained of the lack of a technical adviser as he had a nautical assessor in the Admiralty Court] 'Yes, my Lord, but in the Admiralty Court the Judge is "at sea", which your Lordship never is.'
in *Timothy Healy: Memories and Anecdotes* by Sir Dunbar Plunket Barton

6. JUDGE [whose own son was appearing opposite Healy, to Healy as he rejected the last of many legal submissions with an air of exasperation]: 'Really, Mr Healy, I quite fail to see your point'.
HEALY: 'Of course you do, my Lord, for the son is in your eyes.'
Attrib.

Fr Brendan Hoban

7. We have too many priests in Ireland. Everywhere we go we're tripping over each other.
The Irish Times, August 1993

Denis Johnston

8. It is not fair, my friend. It is a lie that is told to us poor fools who, like the bath-keepers' ass, are content to bring home the fuel that keeps our master's fires alight, and live ourselves on the smell of the smoke.
The Golden Cuckoo

1. Whether the times be hard or good, I have noticed that pimps and jobbers dine better than honest craftsmen should, and that the same cold wind blows through an empty purse.
The Golden Cuckoo

2. Still fishing the waters of a dry well, eh?
The Moon in the Yellow River

3. In most countries the political idealist is merely a bore, but here he has a disconcerting tradition of action. He usually has his own Government and his own army as well, you see.
The Moon in the Yellow River

4. It's my father's fault, he calls me a little slut, but I think it's calling people things that makes them it, don't you?
The Moon in the Yellow River

5. My father says that education poisons the mind, but I say he was educated himself, so his mind must be poisoned, and if it's poisoned, how can he know what's good for me?
The Moon in the Yellow River

James
Joyce

---

6. Makes them feel more important to be prayed over in Latin.
Ulysses

7. More room if they buried them standing.
Ulysses

8. It is a symbol of Irish art. The cracked lookingglass of a servant.
Ulysses

9. – When I makes tea, I makes tea, as old mother Grogan said. And when I makes water, I makes water . . .
– So I do, Mrs Cahill, says she. Begob, ma'am, says Mrs Cahill, God send you don't make them in the one pot.
Ulysses

10. – I just wanted to say, he said. Ireland, they say, has the honour of being the only country who never persecuted the jews. Do you know that? No. And do you know why?
　He frowned sternly on the bright air.
– Why, sir? Stephen asked, beginning to smile.
– Because she never let them in, Mr Deasy said solemnly.
Ulysses

11. Mr Kernan said with solemnity:
– *I am the resurrection and the life*. That touches a man's inmost heart.
– It does, Mr Bloom said.
　Your heart perhaps but what price the fellow in the six feet by two with his toes to the daisies? No touching that. Seat of the affections. Broken heart. A pump

after all, pumping thousands of gallons of blood every day. One fine day it gets bunged up and there you are. Lots of them lying around here: lungs, hearts, livers. Old rusty pumps: damn the thing else. The resurrection and the life. Knocking them all up out of their graves. Come forth, Lazarus! And he came fifth and lost the job. Get up! Last day! Then every fellow mousing around for his liver and his lights and the rest of his traps. Find damn all of himself that morning. Pennyweight of powder in a skull. Twelve grammes one pennyweight. Troy measure.
Ulysses

1. – Are you a strict t. t.? says Joe.
– Not taking anything between drinks, says I. . . .

So we went around by the Linenhall barracks and the back of the courthouse talking of one thing and another. Decent fellow Joe when he has it but sure like that he never has it.
Ulysses

2. Ah! Ow! Don't be talking! I was blue mouldy for the want of that pint. Declare to God I could hear it hit the pit of my stomach with a click.
Ulysses

3. – Paddy Dignam dead? says Alf.
– Ay, says Joe.
– Sure I'm after seeing him not five minutes ago, says Alf, as plain as a pikestaff.

– Who's dead? says Bob Doran.
– You saw his ghost then, says Joe, God between us and harm.
– What? says Alf. Good Christ, only five . . . What? . . and Willy Murray with him, the two of them near whatdoyoucallhim's . . . What? Dignam dead?
– What about Dignam? says Bob Doran. Who's talking about . . .?
– Dead! says Alf. He is no more dead than you are.
– Maybe so, says Joe. They took the liberty of burying him this morning anyhow.
– Paddy? says Alf.
– Ay, says Joe. He paid the debt of nature, God be merciful to him.
– Good Christ! says Alf.
Begob he was what you might call flabbergasted.
Ulysses

4. So then the citizen begins talking about the Irish language and the corporation meeting and all to that and the shoneens that can't speak their own language and Joe chipping in because he stuck someone for a quid and Bloom putting in his old goo with his twopenny stamp that he cadged off Joe and talking about the Gaelic league and the antitreating league and drink, the curse of Ireland. Antitreating is about the size of it. Gob, he'd let you pour all manner of drink down his throat till the Lord would call him before you'd ever see the froth of his pint. And one night I went in with a fellow into one of their musical evenings,

song and dance about she could get up on a truss of hay she could my Maureen Lay, and there was a fellow with a Ballyhooly blue ribbon badge spiffing out of him in Irish and a lot of colleen bawns going about with temperance beverages and selling medals and oranges and lemonade and a few old dry buns, gob, flahoolagh entertainment, don't be talking. Ireland sober is Ireland free. And then an old fellow starts blowing into his bagpipes and all the gougers shuffling their feet to the tune the old cow died of. And one or two sky pilots having an eye around that there was no goings on with the females, hitting below the belt.
Ulysses

1. And off with him and out trying to walk straight. Boosed at five o'clock. Night he was near being lagged only Paddy Leonard knew the bobby, 14 A. Blind to the world up in a shebeen in Bride street after closing time, fornicating with two shawls and a bully on guard, drinking porter out of teacups. And calling himself a Frenchy for the shawls, Joseph Manuo, and talking against the catholic religion and he serving mass in Adam and Eve's when he was young with his eyes shut who wrote the new testament and the old testament and hugging and smugging. And the two shawls killed with the laughing, picking his pockets the bloody fool and he spilling the

porter all over the bed and the two shawls screeching laughing at one another. How is your testament? Have you got an old testament? Only Paddy was passing there, I tell you what. Then see him of a Sunday with his little concubine of a wife, and she wagging her tail up the aisle of the chapel, doing the little lady. Jack Mooney's sister. And the old prostitute of a mother procuring rooms to street couples. Gob, Jack made him toe the line. Told him if he didn't patch up the pot, Jesus, he'd kick the shite out of him.
Ulysses.

2. Myler dusted the floor with him, says Alf . . . Handed him the father and mother of a beating. See the little kipper not up to his navel and the big fellow swiping. God, he gave him one last puck in the wind. Queensbury rules and all, made him puke what he never ate.
Ulysses

3. They believe in rod, the scourger almighty, creator of hell upon earth and in Jacky Tar, the son of a gun, who was conceived of unholy boast, born of the fighting navy, suffered under rump and dozen, was scarified, flayed and curried, yelled like bloody hell, the third day he arose again from the bed, steered into haven, sitteth on his beamend till further orders whence he shall come to drudge for a living and be paid.
Ulysses

1. The citizen said nothing only cleared the spit out of his gullet and, gob, he spat a Red bank oyster out of him right in the corner.
Ulysses

2. – You know Simon Dedalus? he asked at length.
– I've heard of him, Stephen said.
   Mr Bloom was all at sea for a moment, seeing the others evidently eavesdropping too.
– He's Irish, the seaman bold affirmed, staring still in much the same way and nodding. All Irish.
– All too Irish, Stephen rejoined.
Ulysses

3. 'O, the night in the Camden Hall when the daughters of Erin had to lift their skirts to step over you as you lay in your mulberrycoloured, multicoloured, multitudinous vomit!'
   'The most innocent son of Erin for whom they ever lifted them.'
Ulysses

4. Cousin Stephen, you will never be a saint. Isle of saints. You were awfully holy, weren't you? You prayed to the Blessed Virgin that you might not have a red nose. You prayed to the Devil in Serpentine avenue that the fubsy widow in front might lift her clothes still more from the wet street.
Ulysses

5. Richard is coming tonight to the vice-chancellor's dinner. The fatted calf will be eaten: roast, I hope.
Exiles

6. I printed mystical books in dozens:
I printed the table-book of Cousins
Though (asking your pardon) as for the verse
'Twould give you a heartburn on your arse:
I printed folklore from North to South
By Gregory of the Golden Mouth:
I printed poets, sad, silly and solemn:
I printed Patrick What-do-you-Colm:
I printed the great John Millicent Synge
Who soars above on an angel's wing
In the playboy shift that he pinched as swag
From Maunsel's manager's travelling bag.

Shite and onions! Do you think I'll print
The name of the Wellington Monument,
Sydney Parade and Sandymount tram,
Downes's cakeshop and Williams's jam?
Gas from a Burner

7. Poor sister Scotland! Her doom is fell;

She cannot find any more Stuarts
   to sell.
Gas from a Burner

1. In the porch of my printing
   institute
The poor and deserving prostitute
Plays every night as catch-as-
   catch-can
With her tight-breeched British
   artilleryman
And the foreigner learns the gift
   of the gab
From the drunken draggletail
   Dublin drab.
Gas from a Burner

2. But I owe a duty to Ireland:
I hold her honour in my hand,
This lovely land that always sent
Her writers and artists to
   banishment
And in a spirit of Irish fun
Betrayed her own leaders, one by
   one.
'Twas Irish humour, wet and
   dry,
Flung quicklime into Parnell's
   eye;
'Tis Irish brains that save from
   doom
The leaky barge of the Bishop of
   Rome
For everyone knows the Pope
   can't belch
Without the consent of Billy
   Walsh.
Gas from a Burner

3. But all these men of whom I
   speak
Make me the sewer of their
   clique.

That they may dream their
   dreamy dreams
I carry off their filthy streams
For I can do those things for
   them
Through which I lost my diadem,
Those things for which
   Grandmother Church
Left me severely in the lurch.
Thus I relieve their timid arses,
Perform my office of Katharsis.
The Holy Office

4. Where they have crouched and
   crawled and prayed
I stand, the self-doomed, unafraid,
Unfellowed, friendless and alone,
Indifferent as the herring-bone,
Firm as the mountain ridges
   where
I flash my antlers on the air.
The Holy Office

5. [Of John Stanislaus Joyce]
I was very fond of him always,
being a sinner myself, and even
liked his faults.
Letters

6. There is a keen climber called
   Sykes
Who goes scrambling through
   ditches and dykes
To skate on his scalp
Down the side of an alp
Is the kind of diversion he likes.
in *James Joyce* by Richard
Ellman

7. Newly billed for each wickeday
perfumance. Somndoze
massinees. By arraignment,
childream's hours, expercatered.
Finnegans Wake

1. He was grey at three, like sygnus the swan, when he made his boo to the public and barnacled up to the eyes when he repented after seven . . . He was down with the whopping laugh at the age of the loss of reason the whopping first time he prediseased me.
Finnegans Wake

2. He even ran away with himself and became a farssonerite, saying he would far sooner muddle through the hash of lentils in Europe than meddle with Irrland's split little pea.
Finnegans Wake

Stanislaus Joyce

3. I was exasperated by the obstinate waste over a period of seventeen years of such original talent in order to produce in the end the world's masterpiece of strenuous inertia, a kind of cross-word puzzler's bible. For *Finnegans Wake* is not only unreadable but unprintable, as the thousand odd misprints after the first edition prove beyond dispute. I was there to prevent him, so to speak, from jumping off a roof in order to find out whether it hurts.
in *Irish Literary Portraits* by W. R. Rodgers

Maurice (Kruger) Kavanagh

4. I took the fairies out of old men's ears, I took the ribbons off the pigs and the pigs out of the parlours. I shot down drunken Paddies trailing their coats on the road. I left the shamrocks and most of the Blarney but Kathleen Mavourneen hit the screen minus a lot of whiskey, a lot of shillelaghs and a lot of blood.
in *Irish Rogues, Rascals and Scoundrels* by Padraic O'Farrell

Patrick Kavanagh

5. Among the wedding-party there had been a melodeon but no melodeon-player. However, one of the boys pulled the music-box in and out and nobody minded the absence of harmony.
The Green Fool

6. We were about twenty boys and there was only one girl. She was well danced.
The Green Fool

7. It wasn't considered manly to feel any poetic emotion. If a scene was beautiful you didn't say so. A man in love with anything was daft.
The Green Fool

1. At cramming children with religion our teachers had few equals. For weeks before a religious examination, nothing was taught but the catechism; which same had the result of nearly driving all orthodox piety out of me forever.
The Green Fool

2. They knew that all the good things of the earth are the cheapest, and the least thought of. They didn't know that the National Galleries and Libraries, being free to all, have the fewest customers.
The Green Fool

3. I used to hear people saying that God never sends a mouth but he sends something to fill it. A true saying only that it seemed to me – God sometimes sends the mouthful to the wrong address.
The Green Fool

4. Everybody was poor and proud. My parents didn't know anything to be proud of, so they just carried on.
The Green Fool

5. Though little fields and scraping poverty do not lead to grand flaring passions, there was plenty of fire and an amount of vicious neighbourly hatred to keep us awake.
The Green Fool

6. Our clock was dependable, never more than half an hour fast or slow. In any case time hardly mattered much. The sun rose and set in a land of dreams whether the clocks were right or wrong.
The Green Fool

7. The people didn't want a poet, but a fool, yes they could be doing with one of those.
The Green Fool

8. Being made a fool of is good for the soul. It produces a sensitivity of one kind or other; it makes a man into something unusual, a saint or a poet or an imbecile.
The Green Fool

9. That riotous little village
That never was surpassed
For shooting, loot and pillage
Is peaceful now at last.
Collected Poems

10. Once upon a time there was a boy of eighteen who lived in a little house in the country. His father was a hot-tempered man and his mother a wise woman. The boy was as lazy a boy as ever slept on a headland in the sunlight of a June afternoon.
Irish Press, June 1943

11. [Of George Russell] He was the first man who published and paid for a poem of mine, and I was astonished when I got a guinea from him, from *The Irish Statesman*. I didn't meet him actually when he was editing *The Irish Statesman*, I met him after it closed. I met him as a country

gobshite, rather pretending, and I didn't meet him honestly, sincerely, though I recognised him as a great and holy man.
BBC Interview, 1946

1. He called into the pub where the poets who did not write met on Monday and Thursday evenings. There they were all of them sitting praising each other and talking literature all the time.
By Night Unstarred

2. Literary weeds are sometimes popular. Suspicion haunts the book which sells ten thousand copies. In our world ten thousand perceptive readers is an optimism too large for ears of ordinary credulity.
The Irish Times, 1940

3. In every country inarticulate frustration uses whatever weapons are handiest against the creative writer. For a quarter of a century the most potent weapon against the writer in this country has been the 'revival' of Gaelic as a written language. Men with such Irish names as de Valera and Blythe talk of it as the 'badge of nationhood' and have the audacity to speak of writers named O'Connor, O'Faolain, O'Donnell, O'Flaherty as 'Anglo-Irish' writers.
The Bell, 1948

4. The problem that confronts me here
Is to be eloquent yet sincere

Let myself go rip and not go phoney
In an inflated testimony.
Auditors In

5. To those of us who cannot abide the theatre with its flatulent pieties, its contrivances and its lies, 'Waiting for Godot' is a wonderful play.
The Irish Times, January 1956

John B.
Keane

6. 'He is the saviour of our country, the greatest Irishman since Saint Patrick'.
   'But Saint Patrick wasn't an Irishman,' I protested.
   'Neither was Dev,' he whispered triumphantly.
Letters of a Civic Guard

7. Dáil Éireann is the only place in Ireland where the Civil War is still going on.
Many Young Men of Twenty

8. 'There are two kinds of priests,' he declared. 'There are the priests who made themselves and the kind who are made by their mothers.'
Letters of an Irish Parish Priest

9. A looking-glass does nothing for me but I do have a face which reacts favourably to a glass with a drink in it.
The Power of the Word

1. Of course I'm a heavy drinker. Even as a baby I was a nipple tippler.
The Power of the Word

2. He was that kind of critic who loathed sustained applause at the final curtain. His conclusion was that if everybody clapped it had to be common. He would have liked total lack of recognition for the work so that he alone might be credited with the discovery of a new talent.
The Power of the Word

3. He is a true local. Everything local is anathema to him.
The Power of the Word

4. When asked a question she would first scratch some part of her anatomy as if she was consulting a reference book.
The Power of the Word

5. This fish, like life, is just a cod no matter what the sauce suggests.
The Power of the Word

6. Given the unlikely options of attending a funeral or a sex orgy the dyed-in-the-wool Celt will always opt for the funeral.
The Power of the Word

7. Virginity is very like a souvenir: priceless to its proprietor but often worth considerably less in the open market.
The Power of the Word

8. He's a devout hoor all right. He won't be happy till he's crucified.
The Power of the Word

9. Ireland is a nation of Catholics and Protestants, many of them Christians.
The Power of the Word

10. If Caligula could make a consul of his horse why should anybody be surprised if a politician makes an ass of himself?
The Power of the Word

11. The truly modern man is he who has never used anything but toilet paper.
The Power of the Word

12. 'A good stick makes for a good dog.' Sergeant Murnaghan of Boherlahan once told him. 'That is why,' the Sergeant went on, 'dogs attack postmen but never civic guards. We have batons; postmen don't.'
Durango

13. 'I like drink, particularly whiskey. Not only do I like the taste of it but I also like the look of it and I like the gurgle of it when it's poured from a bottle.'
Durango

14. 'I fantasise about whiskey the way other men fantasise about women.'
Durango

15. There is nothing as consoling or sustaining to the half-drunken

imbiber as the presence of a whiskey bottle more full than it is empty.
Christmas Tales

1. There are few snores with the depth and resonance of whiskey snores. They rebounded from the walls and filled the kitchen to overflowing. The only danger to the whiskey snorer is that, more often than not, his slumber is disrupted by one of his own creations.
Christmas Tales

2. Some people had no choice but to be honest while others didn't have the opportunity to be dishonest.
Christmas Tales

3. After his third whiskey and chaser of bottled stout he was assumed into that piquant if temporary state which only immoderate consumption of alcohol can induce.
Christmas Tales

4. He was never possessed of the mettle to refuse drink when kindly souls insisted he partake.
Christmas Tales

5. She had somehow mistaken him for the driver of the jam van. In fact he could be mistaken for anybody. He had that kind of face. A woman once gave him a pound to say Mass. He had been wearing a dark suit on the occasion.
Christmas Tales

Jeremiah Keller

6. [On seeing a pompous blockhead taking his seat on the bench] 'What's Newton worth when one sees Mayne rising by his gravity and Keller sinking by his levity?'
in *John Philpot Curran* by Leslie Hale

John Maurice Kelly

7. The consequence after sixty years [of a bloated Irish public service] is a little like the reverse of Joyce's ugly and cruel image of Ireland as an old sow devouring her young. If there must be a sow in the simile, she is lying, panting, exhausted by her own weight, and being rent by a farrow of cannibal piglets.
Belling the Cats: Selected Speeches and Articles, ed. John Fanagan

8. It [the National Enterprise Agency] is not simply a pig in a poke, because at least while you cannot see the pig, you can see there is something wiggling in there. This is a poke with nothing in it but air, so far as one can judge. There is no sign of life at all in it.
Belling the Cats: Selected Speeches and Articles, ed. John Fanagan

1. What about the local government councillors paid for . . . out of the public purse on their expeditions to international conferences . . . at which the Irish contingent not infrequently outnumbers the rest of the world put together? It was possible for one of my colleagues to report to me on return from one such conference that the centre of Oslo, the night before the conference was to open, presented the aspect of O'Connell Street on the night before an All-Ireland Final.
Belling the Cats: Selected Speeches and Articles, ed. John Fanagan

2. I do not mean to offend the Minister. I sometimes regret that so much of the bitterness has gone out of public life here because occasionally I find it hard to speak as I really think for fear of hurting someone on the far side for whom I have a genuine regard.
Belling the Cats: Selected Speeches and Articles, ed. John Fanagan

3. The Minister over there is the thirteenth stroke of the clock in the Irish political system. He is the one who invites doubt not only about his own authenticity, but about the authenticity of all the other twelve as well. He is a national institution, and I would feel a pang if he lost his seat. He belongs up there at the Hyde Park Corner of the Dáil where the odd bods come in. That is where Deputy Lenihan belongs.
Belling the Cats: Selected Speeches and Articles, ed. John Fanagan

4. If Deputy Kemmy thinks he has heard the limit of Deputy FitzGerald's range he is in for a surprise. If Deputy FitzGerald reverts to the form he showed in the Twentieth Dáil, he will make the acquaintance of Deputy FitzGerald's ranting and raving up and down the scale, like a coloratura foghorn, which could be heard out in the street.
Belling the Cats: Selected Speeches and Articles, ed. John Fanagan

5. I am sorry to say, and I hope it will not be misunderstood, that I detect in the way that visit [of Margaret Thatcher and her Ministers] was reported in the press a certain strain of that awful paddyism which has been our curse. There is a certain note of self-congratulation because as many as four Englishmen travelled over. The gentry had looked into the gate lodge, and not only the master of the house but his dowager mother-in-law as well, and had admired the stove.
Belling the Cats: Selected Speeches and Articles, ed. John Fanagan

1. Mr Haughey, if asked about what he sees as the shape of a Northern solution, will talk airily about an 'all-party, round-table conference'. Why should Unionists – who did not even come to the harmless talking-shop at the Forum – attend such a conference? Would any of us attend a conference which proposed to bury the Irish Republic and was meeting merely to discuss the funeral arrangements?
Belling the Cats: Selected Speeches and Articles, ed. John Fanagan

2. The Irish Title of this Bill [to establish a Dublin Transport Authority] is An Bille un Iompras Bhaile Átha Cliath. That is a good one. I often think of the weary heroes in Rannóg and Aistriúcháin in the House slaving for a lifetime – I have to say with amazing skill and perseverance – to turn the inventions of politicans into plausible Irish. Occasionally I think that perhaps one of them may say, 'We'll try this word. It was never used since the world began and never will be used until the world ends, but we'll see if we can wish it on those óinseachs in there and see if they will swallow it.'
Belling the Cats: Selected Speeches and Articles, ed. John Fanagan

Owen
Kelly

3. There are no flies on the Brorn Law. He knows what's going on in high places, and in low ones, too. There's no subject on which he's not an expert, with the possible exception of the Theory of Relativity, and in that case he knows a man who knows all about it.
Kelly's Fancy

4. One thing has always puzzled me about wrong numbers, though. They're never engaged.
Kelly's Fancy

5. There is something splendidly Irish and reassuringly idiotic in staying away from the doctor because of illness.
Kelly's Fancy

6. There's a distinct lack of warmth in fish, unless properly cooked and served with chips.
Kelly's Fancy

7. I once saw a reference written by a man for a job applicant he didn't like but didn't want to refuse, either. It read simply, 'I have known this applicant for twenty years. He does not smoke.'
Kelly's Fancy

8. There's nobody as daft as an educated man once you get him off the subject he was educated in.
Kelly's Fancy

1. Ahead of me two girls in well-filled red skirts and white blouses were pushing a trolley laden with sandwiches and every male head in the vicinity, mine included, was turned in their direction. Except that everyone else was looking at the girls and I was looking at the sandwiches.
Kelly's Fancy

Patrick
Kelly

2. 'In one word I'll give you George Wright,' he said. 'He's on the border-line of genius; but he never trespasses.'
in *The Old Munster Circuit* by Maurice Healy

3. 'Mr Kelly, I don't think that the members of your faith subscribe as generously as that to the support of their religion.' 'Ah, no, me Lord,' replied Paddy, 'but I understand that it takes the devil of a lot of money to save the soul of a Jew!'
in *The Old Munster Circuit* by Maurice Healy

4. 'The Irish Bishops,' he is reported to have remarked, 'are individually virtuous and sapient men, wise in precept and impeccable in practice. But 'tis a great misfortune that they should always fix their meetings for an occasion when the Holy Ghost happens to be engaged elsewhere.'
Attrib. in *The Old Munster Circuit* by Maurice Healy

Benedict
Kiely

5. In this country there are too many priests in too many families. More priests in this country than soldiers in the army. If we entered a world war all we could contribute would be a quota of chaplains.
The Captain with the Whiskers

6. 'In Segully I was. Sightseeing.'
   'Seeing what? Stones and mud? Heather and mountain sheep? Is the man mad? My da owns a farm up there but even he hires a man to go up and look at it.'
The Captain with the Whiskers

7. Teresa chewed caramels with a squelching noise and a manlike or horselike jaw-movement and Dympna said the noise reminded her of the day her brothers had thrown a frog to a ferret on the bridge at Mortell's mill.
Dogs Enjoy the Morning

8. Did you never hear, Martin, you that knows so much of the old ways, of the Kerry farting competitions? Gold cups and red rosettes for the longest and loudest. It's in the nature of the Kerryman to fart. Big men and windy with ignorance.
Dogs Enjoy the Morning

9. In 1969 a hopeful man said to me: 'for the old-fashioned bigot,

Orange or Green, the writing is on the wall.'

But another man, an Omagh cynic, said: 'The old-fashioned bigot can't or won't read.'
All the Way to Bantry Bay

1. They who ruled the seven seas now blow up bridges at Crossmaglen and lesser places little marked on maps.
All the Way to Bantry Bay

2. Every country-reared man knows that anything he ever learned, of good or bad, was learned not in a classroom but while idling along the road from school. It used to be said of a man of partial education that he never went to school but merely met the scholars coming home.
All the Way to Bantry Bay

3. It was the only time I ever pimped in two languages: something that everybody should try once, as part of a liberal education.
All the Way to Bantry Bay

4. There's a story about a zealous young priest, fresh from the seminary and new to the place and the people, who noticed after a while that a considerable number of men on Owey never bothered to cross over to the church on the mainland to go to confession. So he crossed to the island and cornered the laddoes and asked them why not.

'Well, the way it is, Father,' they say, 'you see the Sound out there.'

'I do.'

'It looks well with the sun on it, but it's not the safest water in the world. The way we look at it is that it's too far to travel for a venial sin, and too dangerous for a mortal sin.'
All the Way to Bantry Bay

5. To burn the roof because you don't like the preacher comes as near to genius as makes no difference.
All the Way to Bantry Bay

6. In the pleasure-grounds between the big house and the weedy lake does there still stand the statue of Socrates to which a zealous novice once addressed his rosary under the impression that he was praying to St Joseph?
All the Way to Bantry Bay

7. As he sipped his way through the long and arduous day he looked and stared moistily and steadily at the shelves of bottles behind the bar, and spoke to nobody, and we all, the locals, left him in the peace that he clearly desiderated. It seems a better word to use in relation to him than merely: desired.
All the Way to Bantry Bay

8. In the inner room overheated hundreds sit on top of each other and suffer from ballads. Ah, the

Irish must love music or they wouldn't endure so much for it. God be with days when a man could talk and have a drink in peace.
All the Way to Bantry Bay

1. The young man is much concerned about clerical celibacy and contraception. Naturally enough, not clerical contraception.
Nothing Happens in Carmincross

2. FARMER: You left my daughter home that snowy night?
YOUNG MAN: I did, so what?
FARMER: You stopped to talk under the chestnut by the avenue gate?
YOUNG MAN: We did.
FARMER: You peed on the snow and wrote your name in pee?
YOUNG MAN: What if I did?
FARMER: It was in my daughter's handwriting.
Nothing Happens in Carmincross

3. In hospital long ago the man in the bed beside him, a modest poor bastard, had suffered hell in pain and humiliation every time a nurse gave him the catheter. Then one day, for one happy moment, it seemed that the waters, stirred by an angel, were about to flow of their own accord: but just when the sufferer was ready to shout his joy to the ward, in came his maiden aunt or something, all flowers and fruit and lucozade and chocolates, and talked and talked nonstop for an hour, and the man was too polite

to beg for the bottle while she was there: and the fountain, frustrated, sank back into the earth . . . When she finally left, her nephew had to call for the catheter in a voice cracked with agony and shame. There is a tide in the affairs of men. It must at least be painful to be a perpetual pisser.
Nothing Happens in Carmincross

4. . . . worked for a while at the building of Clanabogan Church. One day the vicar said to him: 'What height do you think the steeple should be?' 'The height of nonsense like your sermons,' said Martin, and got the sack for his wit.
God's Own Country

5. There was a poltergeist once in a farmhouse in these mountains, and the police decided to investigate the queer happenings, and didn't an ass's collar come flying across the room to settle around the sergeant's neck. Due to subsequent ridicule the poor man had to be transferred to Dublin.
God's Own Country

Patrick
Leary

6. Beneath this stone lies
   Katherine, my wife,
In death my comfort, and my
   plague through life.
Oh, liberty! but soft, I must not
   boast,

She'll haunt me else, by jingo,
   with her ghost.
Gravestone inscription in Belfast

J. J.
Lee

1. Perhaps the Irish simply did
not want economic growth? Were
not the Irish renowned for their
dedication to things of the spirit,
for their renunciation of the
temptations of materialism, to
which a decadent Europe, lacking
Hibernian strength of character,
sadly succumbed? It is an
engaging thought, sedulously
cultivated by some of the Irish
themselves . . .
*Ireland 1912 – 1985: Politics and
Society*

2. The Irish may have been
inefficient materialists. That was
not due to any lack of concern
with material gain. If their values
be deemed spiritual, then
spirituality must be defined as
covetousness tempered only by
sloth.
*Ireland 1912 – 1985: Politics and
Society*

3. Is it really possible to defend
the Irish against charges of
slovenliness, selfishness and
general incapacity to think in
terms of the public good when we
look, for instance, at the litter
dump we have made of our little
country – and imagine what a

garbage heap it would be if we
had European population
densities! We must indeed
wonder if it will not be left to a
later generation to break the link
between Paddy and the pig.
Ireland: Towards a Sense of Place

Maurice
Leitch

4. What an old cesspool his mind
had become over the years, but he
had to admit that he did enjoy
trawling in its depths.
Stamping Ground

Seán
Lemass

5. [Asked what was the principal
difference between Fianna Fáil
and Fine Gael] 'Well, the main
difference is that we're in and
they're out.'
Attrib.

Hugh
Leonard

6. Victory celebration! If I smiled,
it is because I have brought down
my own party and put myself out
of office. In my constituency, I
have been hanged in effigy on the
town hall steps, and yet you
believe there is a cause for
jollification.
Parnell and the Englishwoman

1. I confess that the name 'bachelor' sits uneasily on one who has been twice a widower.
Parnell and the Englishwoman

2. Mr Parnell, I am not clever or accomplished or a woman of the world. But I do know that if I were thought to invite you to my home for my own gain and my husband's, all society would applaud. They would smile and be wise and say: That is how affairs are managed. As my husband is so fond of saying, it is a market-place.
Parnell and the Englishwoman

3. If humiliation had shape and substance, hers would be an empty chair.
Parnell and the Englishwoman

4. All I ever seemed to get was the kind of woman who had a special dispensation from Rome to wear the thickest part of her legs below the knees.
Da

5. You're an Irish summer of a man: sunny skies one day and rain the next. For a week or maybe a month you'd be the height of company: you'd make a cat laugh; next thing, there's a face on you like a plateful of mortal sins and you're off out that door as if there was a curtain rod stuck up you. You can get on with no one: a cup of cold water would disagree with you.
A Life

6. I've been a civil servant for long enough to recognise as such the instincts of a customs official. I am not a suitcase to be stared into and ransacked.
A Life

7. They made a mock of you because you were out of step with them, so you got your own back. You stopped walking.
A Life

8. Fine Gael is convinced it's the Red Chinese, and Fianna Fáil, being more intellectually mature, believes it's the Martians.
Time Was

9. Years before, when the last of several still-births had almost killed my mother, a doctor told her that another pregnancy would be fatal. The Church, knowing that celibacy was, in every sense of the world, child's play, gave her the easy choice of chastity or death.
Out after Dark

10. Just as a cat will leap on the lap of the one person in the room who hates animals, I have always and disastrously been a magnet for my natural enemies.
Out after Dark

11. Ambrose Flood had a model railway, but none of us ever saw it, for it was under the floorboards of his bedroom. It was a Tube train, and Ambrose, who was literal-minded, believed that

it should accordingly be kept underground or at least out of sight.
Out after Dark

1. Everyone enjoyed the Thursday sermon. On that one evening in the year the parishioners could hear sex being talked about without worrying that it might be a sin to listen.
Out after Dark

2. . . . the birth of twins to a girl whose name, Honor, was in the circumstances inappropriate, given that the father was unknown, unhonoured (except in the punning sense) and conspicuously unsung.
Out after Dark

3. Sex, as we all knew, was the worst sin of all, but a single biological mishap could be borne stoically. Twins, however, were not to be glossed over.
Out after Dark

4. I was, as I have said, a snob, and as such clung to the belief – and, to my continued happiness, still cling to it – that in life there exist two classes: first class and no class.
Out after Dark

5. One by one, the cats make themselves comfortable, sitting in the charmed circles of their tails that are like ribbons on Christmas packages.
Rover and Other Cats

6. Priscilla says nothing, perhaps because of an acute personal problem, and it is that in spite of a name as feminine as crinolines or the colour pink, he is in fact a he. And when a chap is addressed as Prissie for short, he thinks twice before putting in his interference.
Rover and Other Cats

7. Its tail was a plume of such magnificence that it almost wore the cat.
Rover and Other Cats

8. Most of our Irish friends liked to drink to excess, on the principle that otherwise they might as well not drink at all.
Rover and Other Cats

9. One knows where one is with a drunk, but teetotalism in an Irishman is unnatural; if it is not checked, he becomes unpredictable and repays watching.
Rover and Other Cats

10. An Irishman will always soften bad news, so that a major coronary is no more than a 'bad turn' and a near-hurricane that leaves thousands homeless is 'good drying weather'.
Rover and Other Cats

11. I have often put to myself the question: what is a cat for? This is as futile an exercise as asking

what laughter is for.
Rover and Other Cats

1. My wife and I have always been law-abiding; she, because she is Belgian, whereas my own motive is the more universal one of cowardice.
Rover and Other Cats

2. He was Welsh but, happily, he did not sing.
Rover and Other Cats

3. Ireland is so hard up for celebrities that it wildly over-uses the few it has, and, as far as her treasured privacy was concerned, I was as much a local landmark as the proverbial begging ass.
Rover and Other Cats

4. It is wrong to think that a cat does not care whether you dislike it or not. A woman of beauty will walk into a restaurant or down the aisle of a theatre knowing, without seeming to look, whose head does not turn at her passing. She is like the archetypal actor who may receive a hundred admiring notices, and yet will take to heart only the single bad one. A cat is similarly an elegant, intuitive, self-possessed female (whatever its sex); it instinctively knows its public from its critics.
Rover and Other Cats

5. Out of a sense of self-preservation I like to have an extra cat in hand for a rainy day.
Rover and Other Cats

Robert
Lynd

6. Sir Edward Carson himself became a furious Nationalist – for Serbs.
Common Sense about Little Nations

7. On a Twelfth of July holiday I had marched with the Belfast Orangemen (not as one of them, alas, but as a stranger!) out to the field of assembly, and there, amid the colours and excited din of loyalty, had seen a stall of trotters bearing the motto: 'Liberty, Equality, and Pigs' Feet'.
Irish and English

8. John Brown never fought half so well for the slaves as John Brown's body did.
Irish and English

9. The loneliness of a man entirely surrounded by women and children surpasses even the loneliness of a man isolated in the middle of the Sahara.
The Shy Fathers

10. No man may be able to add a cubit to his stature, but he has an uneasy suspicion that the eyes of other people's children may be able to take several cubits off him.
The Shy Fathers

11. It is better that the pocket should serve the stomach than that the stomach should serve the pocket. Every child who has ever

broken into its own money-box knows this.
The Money-Box

1. It is a nice point in ethics whether it is dishonest to rob one's own money-box.
The Money-Box

2. There is no six-hour day for the betting man. He is the drudge of chance for every waking hour. He is enviable only for one thing. He knows what to talk about to barbers.
The Betting Man

Nell McCafferty

3. Next time a man says you have a great pair of legs, take off your tights and strangle him.
The Irish Times, 10 October 1980

Tom McDevitt

4. Fast food was something you ate during Lent.
BBC TV, 1993

Patrick MacGill

5. The girls at the school preferred to answer their Catechism in unison, the whole class swaying from side to side as they chanted. Now and again when stopped in the swing they would forget every word of the answer and find themselves in a fix similar to that of dancers in a six hand reel when the fiddle strings break.
Glenmornan

6. 'I was never stingy, for what is the good of being near-going and close-fisted? Greed puts wrinkles in the soul as well as on the forehead.'
Glenmornan

7. 'I'm not a man to take the pledge as long as I can carry a wee drop aisy. What's the good iv a pledge to me anyway? What I can't be, be nature, I'm not going to be, be obligation.'
Glenmornan

8. Oiney gave out the prayers in Irish. Responses were made in that language by the old and in English by the young people of twenty or thereabouts. The children from the school answered in Irish, now a compulsory language in its own country.
Glenmornan

Patrick McGinley

9. 'Professionalism is a great killer of spontaneity,' Joey said. 'Bosco is a professional. To him one sick man is as good as another. They all provide occasions for performing corporal works of mercy.'
The Red Men

1. He was handicapped by his determination to consider one possibility as valid as the next. He probably had a literary phrase for it. All it meant was that though he'd got a first at university he'd get a third in life.
The Red Men

2. Jack used to say that there were two types of men: those who'd been disappointed in their first kiss and those who'd been overwhelmed by it. 'You recover from the second condition but there's no getting over the first,' he'd say with an ambiguous grin.
The Red Men

3. 'I want him to recover,' Cookie repeated.
'So do I – up to a point. If I knew he would disinherit me on recovery tomorrow, I'm afraid I should vote for a quiet and easy exit today. I'm being frank because I abhor humbug, my dear Cookie. Humbug is a means of ensuring that other people think well of us. Unfortunately we must also contrive to think well of ourselves.'
The Red Men

4. 'You could travel. You've never seen the city. It's a marvellous and sinful place.'
'What's the good in seeing other people sinning?'
The Red Men

5. 'I don't like shouting and I don't like bluster,' Cookie replied.
'A good hotel-manager must be able to lose his temper. Otherwise how can he control a bone-idle staff?'
'He could talk quietly and carry a big cudgel.'
'You must be seen to lose your temper. I've been seen to lose mine more often than I've actually lost it. The knack is to lose your temper only when all about you are keeping theirs.'
The Red Men

Medbh McGuckian

6. What is more beautiful than
      potatoes in bloom?
A red-head swinging poteen from
      her breasts,
A smuggler from the cradle, with
      no character to lose,
She gives no dry bargains, she's
      the dough in the still.
Single Ladies

7. Once a man gets land, he loses his thirst.
Single Ladies

8. He says it's unlucky to widen
      the house,
And leaves the gate-posts holding
      up the fairies.
Single Ladies

Walter Macken

9. 'I like sheep. They are good companions. They're a bit

contrary, but you get to know them, and be able to shepherd them. Not like humans. Humans will go back on you no matter how you train them.'
The Bogman

1. 'Mebbe just once to give away a hundred pounds would be more exciting than saving it up,' said Peder.
The Bogman

Bernard
McLaverty

2. 'You say you're from here,' he said. 'If you don't mind me asking, which side are you on?'
   'I'm sort of in the middle.'
   'That can't help.'
   'Well I was born nothing – but a Protestant nothing and I married a Catholic nothing and so I'm now a mixture of nothing. I hate the whole thing. I couldn't give a damn.'
A Time to Dance

3. 'We sort of went together for a while.'
   'You mean he didn't pay.'
   'That kind of thing.'
A Time to Dance

4. His mother had called him Nelson because she said she thought that his father had been a seafaring man.
A Time to Dance

Mícheál
Mac Liammóir

5. Moderation is fatal. Too much is as good as a banquet, enough is as bad as a meal.
An Oscar of No Importance

6. I was at home again: if it wasn't Dublin, it was Cork or Limerick. It must be: for where else would there be a large-sized parish priest sitting in the wings on a kitchen chair?
An Oscar of No Importance

7. [Of Belfast] Impossible to fathom why I like this city but I do. Admittedly a cold, ugly sort of place, even in this radiant northern April, its setting of windy mountains and dark shipyards blotched with *fin-de-siècle* mansions and fussy streets full of plate-glass and cake shops and trams, but there's something about it all, its fantastic practicability, its bleak bowler-hatted refusal of the inevitable.
Put Money in Thy Purse

8. All the thoroughly moral women I know, with two notable exceptions, not only plain, but have a bad habit of humming tunes with loud, shrill, and persistent cheerfulness in cars.
Put Money in Thy Purse

9. Have decided that one's first film has all the less attractive

features of the principle of reincarnation. One is born again in pain and gloom, and, accompanied by half-forgotten images of an adult past, one discovers oneself ignominiously as a baby.
Put Money in Thy Purse

1. We Irish are accused eternally of brooding over the images of the past, but in reality it is by the future, more it may be than other people in the world, that we are driven. It is for the vision of a most questionable posterity that we walk out from our homes, that we dream and plot and play the fool, that we suffer and die. We have created a past for ourselves that we may the more clearly see the future of our hearts' desire, and in the continual striving and sacrifice offered up for that future lies perhaps the only Irish virtue.
All for Hecuba

Bryan MacMahon

2. I clearly recall a deputation of holy women calling to the school to interview me. The spokeswoman told me in awesome tones that they had come to ask me to stop the boys from watching the stallions.

Feigning ignorance, 'What stallions?' I asked. 'The stallions that stand in the stables behind the pub every Friday.' 'Stallions? Pubs?' from disingenuous me. 'They're there to serve the mares. The boys watch them, and it's not good for their immortal souls.' I forget exactly how I coped with this. I did nothing, of course. As a boy I had learnt a great deal from those same stables. I thought it more wholesome than much of what passes for sex education today.
The Master

3. To me, humour has the quality of indelibility: this quality connotes the presentation of the unusual in a usual way, or vice versa. Literature presents the novel as commonplace and the commonplace as novel.
The Master

4. Adversity also contains at its core the pricking of action.
The Master

5. Speaking about an old schoolmaster, someone once said to me that a good teacher leaves the print of his teeth on a parish for three generations.
The Master

6. I was then given into the control and care of a bunch of nubile girls in the senior classes. They hugged me and kissed me and pressed me to their bosoms, giving me my first vague consciousness of the secret possibilities of womanhood.
The Master

1. His eyes were wonderful eyes. They were capable of the subtlest flattery by offering you their whites in exchange for your wonders.
The End of the World and Other Stories

2. 'Did you ever hear what the mountainy man said as he looked at his sow?' asked Pompey.
   'What was that?'
   'He said, "God direct me whether I'll ate you or drink you."'
The End of the World and Other Stories

3. A shot in the boundary elms would have startled them; a rat gnawing in the partition would have terrified them. But the remoter phenomena of people's emotions they perfectly understood.
The End of the World and Other Stories

Brinsley
MacNamara

4. That was my ambition always, to see all the young fellows in Ireland in the Force. To think of the peace we'd have then in Ireland.
The Clanking of Chains

5. But sure I often heard my father, the Lord have mercy on him, say that there was nothing so bad for a person of little or no education as to read much.
The Clanking of Chains

6. There was a prophecy prevalent hereabouts that the Orangemen would break loose some day and never stop till they came to the Bridge of Athlone, where an old woman with a stockingful of stones would stop them.
The Clanking of Chains

7. Begad, they're calling me 'The Comic'. Isn't that a devilish name, anyway, to be giving a man of intellect, making him all as one as a circus clown, making even the flesh and blood of him a kind of jeer, and he walking round on his four bones. And it's not even as if I was making a living out of it, like a common whore.
The Clanking of Chains

8. I told you of my plan, that's so simple and so natural, why a child could work it. I'm not going to tell you what it is, but to begin with it would mean converting the Irish people back to Christianity.
The Clanking of Chains

Louis
MacNeice

9. You know I designed the security fence? Well, it's not very easy to make that sort of thing chic, but I think my success is proved by that poor little boy. You

know, the one that got
electrocuted. He wanted to climb
it, I'm told, because he thought it
so pretty. Like something out of a
fairy story – one of those
impregnable castles.
The Administrator

1. You're wrong, Bill, it's the
hardheads like you are dreamers:
you dream of becoming tycoons
as if this were fifty years ago. And
Cabinet Ministers dream of
remaining Cabinet Ministers. And
my wife of course is a dreamer;
she dreams she can put the clock
back or jump on the needle on
the record or keep the eggs soft-
boiled by turning the egg-boiler
round . . .
The Administrator

2. Everything has to happen some
time. But that time is fixed; you
can never jump ahead of it.
The Mad Islands

3. Thirty – I am offered
thirty – thirty pieces of silver. Any
advance on thirty? All done at
thirty? Sold for thirty pieces of
silver. To the gentleman in the
mask. Now my next lot, lot 99, is
rather a mixed bag. I might call it
a lot and a half or maybe a lot and
a wife. It consists of the following
items: one pillar of salt . . .
The Mad Islands

4. Come along there, walk up, I'll
buy all your doubts and
disappointments, your defeated

hopes, your encumberances, I'll
buy all your cares and your
chores, your backbitings and your
second thoughts. Come on up
there, shovel them in – your
hypocrisies and mediocrities,
your outmoded ornaments and
armaments, your half-baked
lumps of dough, your half-formed
castles in the air, your stillborn
babies, your unhappy pasts.
The Mad Islands

5. This was never my town,
I was not born nor bred
Nor schooled here and she will
    not
Have me alive or dead
But yet she holds my mind
With her seedy elegance,
With her gentle veils of rain
And all her ghosts that walk
And all that hide behind
Her Regency façades –
The catcalls and the pain,
The glamour of her squalor,
The bravado of her talk.
The Last Ditch

6. Time was away and somewhere
    else,
There were two glasses and two
    chairs
And two people with one pulse
(Somebody stopped the moving
    stairs):
Time was away and somewhere
    else.
The Last Ditch

7. The camels crossed the miles
    of sand

That stretched around the cups
and plates;
The desert was their own, they
planned
To portion out the stars and
dates:
The camels crossed the miles of
sand.
The Last Ditch

1. Will he come to pester,
To cringe or to bluster,
A promise in his palm,
Or a gun in his holster?
The Last Ditch

2. The land of scholars and saints:
Scholars and saints my eye, the
land of ambush,
Purblind manifestoes, never-
ending complaints,
The born martyr and the gallant
ninny;
The grocer drunk with the drum,
The land-owner shot in his bed,
the angry voices
Piercing the broken fanlight in
the slum,
The shawled woman weeping at
the garish altar.
Autumn Journal

3. Drums on the haycocks,
drums on the harvest, black
Drums in the night shaking the
windows:
King William is riding his white
horse back
To the Boyne on a banner.
Thousands of banners, thousands
of white
Horses, thousands of Williams

Waving thousands of swords and
ready to fight
Till the blue sea turns to orange.
Autumn Journal

4. Why do we like being Irish?
Partly because
It gives us a hold on the
sentimental English
As members of a world that never
was,
Baptised with fairy water;
And partly because Ireland is
small enough
To be still thought of with a
family feeling.
Autumn Journal

5. A city built upon mud;
A culture built upon profit;
Free speech nipped in the bud,
The minority always guilty.
Autumn Journal

Sean
Mac Reamoinn

6. Outside every thin woman,
there is a fat man trying to get in.
Attrib.

J. P.
Mahaffy

7. They used to say of me when I
was a tutor that you could drop
me anywhere in Ireland and I
should not be more than three
miles from my dinner.
in *Mahaffy* by Stanford and
MacDowell

1. We have taken Oscar Wilde with us, who has of course come round under the influence of the moment from Popery to Paganism, but what his Jesuit friends will say, who supplied the money to land him at Rome, it is not hard to guess. I think it is a fair case of cheating the Devil.
in *Mahaffy* by Stanford and MacDowell

2. There are other things promoted by privacy besides prayer.
in *Mahaffy* by Stanford and MacDowell

3. The BA is like the commission in the army which used to mark the officer and the gentleman, and which is therefore very attractive to those whose claim to the latter is doubtful.
in *Mahaffy* by Stanford and MacDowell

4. The mere making of great and useful discoveries, such as Newton's, though admirable in many ways, do not constitute genius in the strictest sense. All that Newton or most other scientific pioneers have discovered would have been put together or brought out by a number of lesser minds in the process of time.
in *Mahaffy* by Stanford and MacDowell

5. I have spent an evening shut up with a commercial traveller in a remote country inn, and yet by trying honestly to find out what he knew and liked, succeeded in drawing from him a most interesting account of his experiences, first in tea-tasting, then in tea-selling to the Irish peasants in the remote glens of Donegal. What he told me was quite worthy to make an article in a good magazine. Yet a more unpromising subject for a long dialogue could hardly be found. He and I had apparently not a single interest in common. But when the right vein was touched one had to supply nothing but assent, or the occasional question. People said that others found him morose and unapproachable. It was certainly their fault.
in *Mahaffy* by Stanford and MacDowell

6. A man who can say a good thing or make a person appear ridiculous may be so proud of his power that he exercises it at a cost of good taste and even of real humanity. The great wit is often cruel, and even glories in wounding to the quick the sensibilities of others.
in *Mahaffy* by Stanford and MacDowell

7. The most marvellous old man I ever met was after the siege of Paris. It was at a civic banquet given to celebrate our deliverance from having to eat cats and dogs and rats and mice. He was one hundred and eight and as gay as a

lark. But I am sorry to say there were some very wicked French actresses present, and he went away with the worst of them, and was found dead in his bed next morning.

'Well (said one of the company) the moral is, I suppose, beware of French actresses.'

'Ah yes . . . when you are a hundred and eight.'
in *Mahaffy* by Stanford and MacDowell

1. In Ireland the inevitable never happens and the unexpected constantly occurs.
in *Mahaffy* by Stanford and MacDowell

2. An Irish Bull is always pregnant.
in *Mahaffy* by Stanford and MacDowell

3. If anyone is justly described as an old fool, you may rest assured that he was also a young fool.
in *Mahaffy* by Stanford and MacDowell

4. An Irish atheist is one who wishes to God he could believe in God.
in *Mahaffy* by Stanford and MacDowell

5. The most popular speaker is the one who sits down before he stands up.
in *Mahaffy* by Stanford and MacDowell

6. We have no time in Ireland for a man who doesn't waste both his money and his time.
in *Mahaffy* by Stanford and MacDowell

7. There is no country in which sham excuses, political and religious, for appointing incompetent men to responsible posts flourish more signally than in Ireland.
in *Mahaffy* by Stanford and MacDowell

P. J.
Mara

8. [To a journalist about to interview Charles J. Haughey] No oul' Arms Trial shite now!
in *Charlie* by T. Ryle Dwyer

9. *Uno duce, una voce!* In other words, we are having no more nibbling at my leader's bum.
in *Charlie* by T. Ryle Dwyer

Rev. William Frederick
Marshall

10. I'm living in Drumlister
An' I'm gettin' very oul',
I have to wear an Indian bag
To save me from the coul',
The deil a man in this town lan'
Wos claner raired nor me,
But I'm livin' in Drumlister
In clabber to the knee.
'Me an' Me Da'

Brian
Merriman

1. Chaste Eevell, hasten to the
   relief
Of the women of Erin in their
   grief,
Wasting their pains in vain
   endeavour
To meet with mates who elude
   them ever,
Till in the ages is such disparity
We would not touch them except
   from charity.
The Midnight Court

2. My heart is torn and worn with
   grieving,
And my breast distressed with
   restless heaving,
With torture dull and with
   desperation
At the thought of my dismal
   situation,
When I see a bonny and bold
   young blade
With comely features and frame
   displayed,
A sturdy swearer or spanking
   buck,
A sprightly strapper with spunk
   and pluck,
A goodly wopper well made and
   planned,
A gamey walloper gay and grand,
Nimble and brave and bland and
   blithe,
Eager and active and brisk and
   lithe,
Of noted parts and of proved
   precocity,

Sold to a scold or old hidiosity.
The Midnight Court

3. I'm not course or ragged or
   rank of limb,
Not stringy or scraggy or lanky or
   lean
But as fair a female as ever was
   seen,
A pleasing, teasing and tempting
   tart
That might coax and entice the
   coldest heart
The Midnight Court

4. And – that God may judge me!
   only I hate
A scandalous tongue, I could
   relate
Things of that woman's previous
   state
As one with whom every man
   could mate
In any convenient field or gate
As the chance might come to him
   early or late!
The Midnight Court

5. For though everyone talked of
   her carouses
As a scratching post of the public
   houses
That as sure as ever the glasses
   would jingle
Flattened herself to married and
   single,
Admitting no modesty to
   mention,
I never believed but 'twas all
   invention.
The Midnight Court

Christy
Moore

1. Goodbye to the Port and
   Brandy, to the Vodka and the
   Stag,
To the Schmiddic and the Harpic,
   the bottle draught and keg.
As I sat lookin' up at the Guinness
   ad, I could never figure out
How your man stayed up on the
   surfboard after 14 pints of
   stout.
*Delirium Tremens, The Christy
Moore Collection*

2. Everybody needs a break,
Climb a mountain or jump in a
   lake.
Some head off to exotic places,
Others go to the Galway races.
Matti goes to the South of France,
Jim to the dogs, Peter to the
   dance,
A cousin of mine goes potholin',
A cousin of hers loves Joe Dolan.
As the summer comes around
   each year
We go there and they come here.
Some head off to Frijiliana
But I always go to Lisdoonvarna.

The multitudes they flocked in
   throngs
To hear the music and the songs.
On motorbikes and Hiace vans
With bottles, barrels, flagons,
   cans,
Mighty crack and loads of frolics,
Pioneers and alcoholics.
PLAC, SPUC and the FCA,
Free Nicky Kelly and the IRA,
Hairy chests and milk white
   thighs,
Mickey dodgers in disguise,
McGraths, O'Briens, Pippins,
   Cox's,
Massage parlours in horse boxes,
Amhráns, bodhráns, amadáns,
Arab sheiks, Hindu sikhs, Jesus
   freaks,
RTE makin' tapes, takin' breaks,
   throwin' shapes.
This is heaven, this is hell.
Who cares? Who can tell?
Anyone for the last few choc
   ices?
*Lisdoonvarna, The Christy Moore
Songbook*

George
Moore

3. Olive's hair was the colour of
primroses. Her face, with its
pronounced nose, was full of all
the pseudo-classicality of a
cameo. Now the action of
listening had distended the
limbs, and the skirt was cast
into folds that made clear the
movement of the body; the
arms and bosom were moulded
into amorous plenitudes, and
the extremities flowed into
chaste slendernesses, that the
white stocking and loose
convent-shoe could not distort.
In the beautiful framework
nothing was wanting but a
mind.
A Drama in Muslin

1. As they grew old and ugly, the Ladies Cullen had developed an inordinate passion for the conversion of souls. They had started a school of their own in opposition to the National school, which was under the direction of the priest. To obtain a supply of scholars, and to induce the peasants to eat fat bacon on Friday, were good works that could not be undertaken without funds.
A Drama in Muslin

2. I could never quite bring myself to credit that there was a Being far away, sitting behind a cloud, who kept his eye on all the different worlds, and looked after them just as a stationmaster looks after the arrival and departure of trains from some huge terminus.
A Drama in Muslin

3. No danger of cold when you have shammy-leather drawers.
A Drama in Muslin

4. An entire race, a whole caste, saw themselves driven out of their soft, warm couches of idleness, and forced into the struggle for life. The prospect appalled them; birds with shorn wings could not gaze more helplessly on the high trees where they had built, as they thought, their nests out of reach of evil winds. What could they do with their empty brains?

What could they do with their feeble hands?
A Drama in Muslin

5. Dublin is like a racecourse, men come and speak to you and pass on.
A Drama in Muslin

6. Catholic in name, they curse the Pope for not helping them in their affliction; moralists by tradition, they accept at their parties women who parade their lovers to the town from the top of a tram-car. In Dublin there is baptism in tea and communion in a cutlet.
A Drama in Muslin

7. Having nothing to do must be a terrible occupation, and one difficult to fulfil with dignity and honour.
A Drama in Muslin

8. Happy canal! enjoying the Sunday in its own irreproachable fashion. What is this blackness that I see approaching? A boat, and coming to interrupt my pretty meditation! I had hoped that the last went by twenty years ago.
Memoirs of my Dead Life

9. A woman versed in the art of love prepares herself for bed so imperceptibly that any attempts to indicate a stage in her undressing breaks the harmony.
Memoirs of my Dead Life

1. Edward Martyn started the Pro-Cathedral choir, not because he likes choirs, but because he likes choirboys.
As recounted by W. B. Yeats in *Irish Literary Portraits* by W. R. Rodgers

2. His [Douglas Hyde's] volubility was extreme as a peasant's come to ask for a reduction in rent. It was interrupted, however, by Edward [Martyn] calling on him to speak in Irish, and then a torrent of dark, muddied stuff flowed from him, much like the porter which used to come up from Carnacun to be drunk by the peasants on Midsummer nights when a bonfire was lighted. It seemed to me a language suitable for the celebrations of an antique Celtic rite, but too remote for modern use. It had never been spoken by ladies in silken gowns with fans in their hands.
Hail and Farewell 1: Ave

Thomas
Moore

3. My birthday! – what a different sound
That word had in my youthful ears;
And how each time the day comes round,
Less and less white its mark appears.
My Birthday

Anna
Mundon

4. And the lust shall be first.
The Irish Times, February 1993

Kevin
Myers

5. Oh, I know you poor simpletons breathe through your mouths, trail your knuckles on the floor and look on journalists as omniscient fonts of, well, omniscience.
The Irish Times, 25 January 1984

6. [On the suggestion made by Dr Charles Nelson in *Field and Countryside* that shamrock does not exist, but is in the winter resting stage of clover, and would flower if left in your garden] Flowering shamrock – what a revolting suggestion . . . each little lot of shamrock is sold for 50p, which gives [that] acre a crop whose street value is 2 million. And, those chaps growing opium poppies and marijuana up around the North West frontier thought they had it made. They should be growing shamrock. Best Afghan green.
The Irish Times, 5 March 1985

7. Flags and emblems are strange things and are as lethal to toy with as a mercury switch booby trap.
The Irish Times, 6 March 1985

1. . . . we had that divine harbinger of summer – warm rain.
The Irish Times, 3 April 1985

2. [On Good Friday] . . . the days lasts several weeks . . . In my religious days . . . I remember church services lasting a month, or more, and you'd get out of church expecting it to be mid summer with swallows all over the place, only to find it was still the same day, and the middle of the afternoon only.
The Irish Times, 10 April 1985

3. [On EC grant aid to golf in the Donegal-Leitrim-Sligo area] . . . I would have thought all those poor folk who live in the border areas of the North West have enough to worry about without a plague of grim faced, gibbering golfers swarming like tics all over the place, chivvying and chipping and cursing . . .
The Irish Times, 5 May 1985

4. [On the failure of Britain to capitalise on their design classic the Morris Minor, in the same way that Germany did with the VW Beetle] But the British regarded salesmanship as apparently ungentlemanly, the calling of cads, bounders and spivs with loud ties one would never dream of permitting in the officers' mess.
The Irish Times, 26 March 1986

5. [On a sighting of the first swallow in March] Can you imagine what that poor bird has been going through, stamping its tiny feet on tree branches to keep them warm . . . And that poor creature had come all the way from Africa in the expectation that it was coming here to enjoy a bit of summertime.
The Irish Times, 2 April 1986

6. Now there has been an excellent system in recent years . . . by which women are forbidden to play golf on the same terms as men. . . . One can only hope that soon these golf clubs stop discriminating against men, and introduce the necessary ordinances and bye-laws to prevent men from playing as well. A golf-free world, mankind's dream since the dawn of time.
The Irish Times, 2 April 1986

7. [Breast feeding as opposed to bottle feeding] . . . that excellent natural product, on tap, so to speak, wherever mother and child should be at the time . . . replaced by a witch's kit of bottles, powders, thermometers, saucepans and cooker.
The Irish Times, 26 March 1987

8. [On the necessity of including a Saturday night stopover to qualify for APEX price] What is it about Saturday night that so revolutionises airlines' attitudes

to travel? Was some secret quality injected into the sixth day of creation which elevates it into a class of its own, only known to a chosen few, like the scriptures of the Druse?
The Irish Times, 15 April 1987

Conor Cruise
O'Brien

1. I live in Ireland by choice, after experience of living in many other places, and I am happy here. Our neighbours are friendly, our view is beautiful, my political friends are fine upstanding people, my political enemies fascinating in their own way. I don't mind the gossip any more than the rain. The censors are no longer eating writers in the street. We are not as bad as we are painted, especially by ourselves. In fact, I love Ireland, as most Irish people do, with only an occasional fit of the shudders.
States of Ireland

2. In late October 1968 . . . I addressed a large, mainly student audience at Queen's University Belfast on 'Civic Disobedience' . . . I was criticised . . . for mentioning an aspect of reality: the existence of two separate communities, Catholics and Protestants. This was held to be 'irrelevant', a favourite all-purpose student knock-out word

at the time, in Belfast as well as in New York. 'Religion,' one student said, 'is a red herring.' I said if so it was a red herring about the size of a whale.
States of Ireland

3. My wife . . . heard a priest in Dingle, Co. Kerry, deliver a sermon on 'communism and socialism'. The priest gave communism the expected treatment. Then he went on to socialism. 'Socialism,' he said, 'is worse than communism. Socialism is a heresy of communism. Socialists are a Protestant variety of communists.' Not merely communists, but Protestant communists! Not many votes for Labour in Dingle.
States of Ireland

4. A Samuel Ferguson, in Ulster, could interest himself in Ancient Ireland, but not too much in the degenerate descendants of a great Celtic past.
States of Ireland

5. By the time of the Boer War, however, Protestant Ulster was one of the most jingo parts of the Empire, noisily hostile to a people, the Afrikaners, which was in fact very like itself: dourly Protestant, thoroughly besieged, sure of its God-given superiority, slow, suspicious, determined and tough.
States of Ireland

1. Silence and ignorance have their own dynamics. Most of the people of Catholic Ireland, outside Ulster itself, knew little or nothing about the real situation in Ulster. Their political leaders, who did know, did not tell them.
States of Ireland

2. The sinister euphoria of the leader of Sinn Féin even exceeded in intensity the euphoria of so many peace-loving people, over the same event: the signing of the Hillsborough Agreement. And I greatly fear that the leader of Sinn Féin may have had more to be euphoric about than did the framers of the Agreement.
Address to the Friends of the Union

3. I think it fair to say that most people in the Republic do not actually want Northern Ireland. They are simply in the habit of hearing, and of repeating, that Northern Ireland has no right to exist.
Address to the Friends of the Union

4. Mr Mallon has always felt a need to say out loud what he thinks and feels. Mr Hume has never been in the grip of any comparable addiction.
The Independent, March 1994

5. Irishness is not primarily a question of birth or blood or language; it is the condition of being involved in the Irish situation, and usually of being mauled by it.
The New Statesman, 1959

Edna
O'Brien

6. Then he put the light on and I saw what had happened. He had bought me a scarf, and having bought it in a second-hand shop, he had decided to wash it, but washing in his mind was confused with boiling, and the colours had run.
Johnny I Hardly Knew You

7. He had learnt the inevitable: 'What's done is done, what's dead is dead.' Yet he too knew that nothing is utterly dead and the departed leave in us an invisible gong that can strike at any moment.
Johnny I Hardly Knew You

8. His father recommended that he write the correct thing which was to renounce Mother who was mad, being a woman, and to espouse Father who was good and upright, being a man.
Johnny I Hardly Knew You

9. He said he had his muscles under such control that he could make love to twenty-five women in one evening.
Girls in Their Married Bliss

1. 'Have you a black brassiere?'
he said. Of course I had. It's the
only colour you don't have to
wash every four minutes.
London is so filthy you'd be out
of your mind to wear any other
colour.
Girls in Their Married Bliss

2. Baba had green eyes that
drooped at the corners and were
inclined to flashes of wickedness.
An occasional blow from her
husnad gave one or other of those
green eyes a permanent
knowingness, as if at twenty-five
she realised what life was all
about.
Girls in Their Married Bliss

3. 'You may not be educated,' said
I, 'but you're a gombeen at heart.
You'll go far.'
Girls in Their Married Bliss

4. He didn't propose for at least
six dinners and that shook me. I
didn't know whether to be pleased
or offended.
Girls in Their Married Bliss

5. Bills never worried Dada, he
just put them behind plates and
forgot.
The Country Girls

6. But Martha was not ever sad,
unless being bored is a form of
sadness. She wanted two things
from life and she got them –
drink and admiration.
The Country Girls

7. Martha was not mean. She took
pride and vengeance in spending
his money, but like all drinkers
she was reluctant to spend it on
anything other than drink.
The Country Girls

8. She would have liked to be a
nun, it was better than marrying.
Anything was, she thought.
The Country Girls

9. 'It's the colour of my orchid,' I
said and I looked over at my
orchid which was still pinned to
my cardigan. I touched it. Not my
orchid. His. It was soft and
incredibly tender, like the inside
of a flower, and it stirred. It
reminded me when it stirred of a
little black man on top of a
collecting box that shook his head
every time you put a coin in the
box.
The Country Girls

10. I did not sleep. I never do
when I am over-happy, over-
unhappy, or in bed with a strange
man.
The Love Object

Flann
O'Brien

11. My mother I can recall
perfectly. Her face was always red
and sore-looking from bending at
the fire; she spent her life making
tea to pass the time and singing
snatches of old songs to pass the
meantime.
The Third Policeman

1. It [the porter] was manufactured in some town in the south and was known as 'The Wrastler'. If you drank three or four pints of it, it was nearly bound to win.
The Third Policeman

2. 'When I was meditating,' said Old Mathers, 'I took all my sins out and put them on the table, so to speak. I need not tell you it was a big table.'
The Third Policeman

3. This whole State is alive with hoodlums and politicians, and when was there any difference between these two classes?
Stories and Plays

4. He could gaze across the broad valley of the Liffey to the slopes of the Phoenix Park, peacefully. Usually the river was indiscernible but on a sunny morning it could be seen lying like a long glistening spear in the valley's palm. Like a respectable married man, it seemed to be hurrying into Dublin as if to work.
Stories and Plays

5. A man once said to me that he hated blasphemy, but on purely rational grounds. If there is no God, he said, the thing is stupid and unnecessary. If there is, it's dangerous.
Stories and Plays

6. 'One hadn't thought of him as a painter, actually. His work irritates one, you know, so derivative and all that.'
'I do quite definitely agree, but personally I trace his influences more in sorrow than in anger.'
'You mean more in Seurat than in Ingres, old thing.'
The Best of Myles

7. Do engine drivers, I wonder, eternally wish they were small boys?
The Best of Myles

8. By the way, Keats once had a female parrot which he called Tess. 'Toujours la Polly Tess!' he was wont to roar at her in his odder moments.
The Best of Myles

9. My idea is to have the hours altered so that public houses will be permitted to open only between two and five in the morning. This means that if you are a drinking man you'll have to be in earnest about it.
The Best of Myles

10. Keats and Chapman once climbed Vesuvius and stood looking down into the volcano, watching the bubbling lava and considering the sterile ebullience of the stony entrails of the earth. Chapman shuddered as if with cold or fear.
'Will you have a drop of the crater?' Keats said.
The Best of Myles

1. Keats and Chapman once went into a very expensive restaurant and ordered roes of tunny or some such delicacy. The manager explained apologetically that this dish had just gone out of season. Keats, however, insisted and the manager promised 'to see what he could do'. We do not know whether he called in the aid of some other restaurant, but the desired dishes were eventually produced. The two diners gorged themselves delightedly. Then Keats began to hum a tune.

'What's that you're humming,' Chapman asked.

'The last roes of summer,' Keats said pleasantly.
The Best of Myles

2. Take the word 'relegate'. To what must a person be relegated? That obscurity from which he should never have been permitted to emerge.
The Best of Myles

3. In relation to any problem, what commodity of apparently fluid nature is it necessary to hammer out?

A solution.
The Best of Myles

4. Poets don't matter and an odd senseless bit of talk matters little either. What is important is food, money, and opportunities for scoring off one's enemies. Give a man those three things and you won't hear much squawking out of him.
The Best of Myles

5. A lot of nonsense is talked about the sun. Get plenty of fresh air and sunlight, a doctor will tell you. Observe the effect of fresh air and sunlight on flowers. Almost under your eyes they are forced to precocious bloom, now they are already withered and crumbling to dust.
The Best of Myles

6. I suppose he was right when he said there was far too much shop-lifting in Dublin but I am not clear how one calculates what is the right amount of shop-lifting for Dublin. Would we be in a worse mess if there was too little shop-lifting?
The Best of Myles

7. Say I make a 'joke' and it doesn't appeal to you, you are annoyed rather than amused. Annoyed, simply because you haven't yet found out how to unlaugh.
The Best of Myles

8. We are not the men our fathers were. (A good job, in a way. If we were, we would be . . . terribly old.)
The Best of Myles

9. You have been to some very late and boring function. You are going home, you feel you need a drink, you are a gentleman and know nothing whatever about the licensing laws. Naturally you rap at the door of the first pub you see. All is in darkness. The door opens, a head appears, it peeps up

the street and then down; next thing you are whisked in.

'We're supposed to be closed, you know.'
The Best of Myles

Kate
O'Brien

1. In her youth she had tried to be a nun and failed, Heaven knows why.
Mary Lavelle

2. His beauty was deceptive, for though it could promise either sexual or intellectual vitality, according to the imagination that considered it, Dr Lavelle was possessed of neither.
Mary Lavelle

3. In the convention of Mary's upbringing a suitably affianced girl is a happy girl and Mary was therefore by her own conventional Assumption happy.
Mary Lavelle

4. Though he calls them political writings, there are no politics in them. You see, he thinks exactly as I do, that any political organisation, no matter what, is most offensive.
Mary Lavelle

5. You could get to know about birds here – if you wanted to.
The Last of Summer

6. 'All this drinking! No wonder Europe is the way it is!'

'Hitler and Mussolini are teetotallers,' said Angele.
The Last of Summer

7. 'May I have cider?'
'Lord, the stuff people drink!'
The Last of Summer

8. 'You know perfectly well, Dotey,' said Martin, 'that your solicitous Dev doesn't let an immoral rag within three hundred miles of you. This country is Heaven's ante-room,' he said to Angele, 'whether we like the idea or not.'
The Last of Summer

9. His way of courtship was complete subservience, a flow of silly jokes and silly songs, and regular presentations of fine boxes of chocolates.
The Last of Summer

10. 'Are you – are you in love with anyone?'
'No.'
'Have you ever been?'
'From what I read about it – no, I haven't.'
The Last of Summer

11. 'You're on the wrong card again, Jo! Here, let me bet for you!'
'What on earth fun would that be?' said Jo.
The Last of Summer

12. He has about six lines of Homer, and he uses them like a genius.
The Last of Summer

1. 'This national dancing blows the gaff on us, I always think. If you like it proves why Dev is making a success of us. We're a prim, stiff-backed lot!'
The Last of Summer

2. He waltzes like a Protestant curate.
The Last of Summer

3. Dotey was timid and greedy – and both excessively. She had all her life refused responsibility, loathed it and denied it; with equal certainty she had insisted on material comfort. She wanted nothing of life save to be quit of its personal assaults, and to be well fed and well bedded.
The Last of Summer

Seán O'Casey

4. You're hauling on a rope that isn't there!
Cock-a-Doodle Dandy

5. Women is more flexible towards th' ungodly than us men, an' well th' old saints knew it.
Cock-a-Doodle Dandy

6. Softer an' safer than St Patrick's breastplate is a woman's breast to save a man from the slings of life.
Purple Dust

7. What's the advantage of your passing through Oxford if you can't face a bull with a gun in your hand?
Purple Dust

8. The bigger half of Ireland would say that a man's way with a maid must be regulated by his faith an' hers, an' the other half by the way her father makes his livin'.
Red Roses for Me

9. I envy you the handling of a flower by day and of a girl by night.
Within the Gates

10. We'd have free love without fee or license introducing smash-and-grab methods into the holy solicitation of marriage.
The Star Turns Red

11. I can never understand why some workers are ready to fall on their knees the minute a well-dressed cow flits in front of them.
The Star Turns Red

12. I don't know which of you's the bigger bum – him who thinks he's given to heaven, or you who know you're given to drink.
The Bishop's Bonfire

13. There's plenty of men can't sleep in peace at night now unless they know that they have shot somebody.
The Shadow of a Gunman

1. An' you daren't open your mouth, for Kathleen Ni Houlihan is very different now to the woman who used to play the harp an' sing 'Weep on, weep on, your hour is past', for she's a ragin' divil now, an' if you only look crooked at her you're sure of a punch in the eye.
The Shadow of a Gunman

2. When the Tommies have the wind up they let bang at everything they see – they don't give a God's curse who they plug.
The Shadow of a Gunman

3. That's the Irish people all over – they treat a joke as a serious thing and a serious thing as a joke.
The Shadow of a Gunman

4. When we got the makin' of our own laws I thought we'd never stop to look behind us, but instead of that we never stopped to look before us!
Juno and the Paycock

5. You lost your best principle, me boy, when you lost your arm; them's the only sort o' principles that's any good to a workin' man.
Juno and the Paycock

6. Th' Minstrel Boys aren't feelin' very comfortable now. Th' big guns has knocked all th' harps out of their hands.
The Plough and the Stars

7. There's no reason to bring religion into it. I think we ought to have as great a regard for religion as we can, so as to keep it out of as many things as possible.
The Plough and the Stars

8. In my opinion the chief problems the old have to face are three: social, economic, and the young.
Blasts and Benedictions

9. It isn't as if Lady Gregory had given the back of her hand to Ireland, and has left her for another land, as Shaw had done with a laugh, and as Joyce had done with a scornful curse.
Blasts and Benedictions

10. When in a tremor of fear, or in a spasm of ridiculous self-righteousness, we turn up our noses at a 'vulgar' or an 'improper' word, we really repudiate, we even insult, quite a number of impressive persons.
Blasts and Benedictions

11. There are quite a few chaps who think they should be able to get all they want from a girl for a cup of tea and a wafer-biscuit, and are unhappy if they find they have to pay more than what they thought the right market-value for their pleasure.
Blasts and Benedictions

12. It shows what odd things may happen when a pietist ceases to

pray for a moment; how bewildered and lost he becomes because of a first lingerieing glance at lace on a petticoat.
Blasts and Benedictions

1. Oh, I'm findin' out that everyone who wears a cocked hat isn't a Napoleon.
The Silver Tassie

2. Manhandle the lassies of France, if you like, but put on your gloves when you touch a woman that seeketh not the things of the flesh.
The Silver Tassie

3. SUSIE: Will the operation tomorrow be successful?
SURGEON MAXWELl: Oh, of course; very successful.
SUSIE: Do him any good, d'ye think?
SURGEON MAXWELL: Oh, blast the good it'll do him.
The Silver Tassie

4. To carry life and colour to where there's nothing but the sick and helpless is right; but to carry the sick and helpless to where there's nothing but life and colour is wrong.
The Silver Tassie

Frank
O'Connor

5. [Of F. R. Higgins] I used to call him a Protestant with all the vices of a Catholic, if you know

what that means.
in *Irish Literary Portraits* by W. R. Rodgers

6. Even if there were only two men left in the world and both of them had to be saints, they wouldn't be happy even then. One of them would be bound to try and improve the other.
Crab Apple Jelly

7. He was a resourceful chap, and it was he who invented the dockets, valued for so many Hail Marys. The man who lost had to pay up in prayers for the other man's intention. It was an ingenious scheme and it worked admirably.
Crab Apple Jelly

8. 'Ye're always at it. Corpses and graves and people that are dead and gone.'
   'Arrah, why wouldn't we?' she replied, looking down stiffly as she tried to button the open-necked blouse that revealed her old breast. 'Isn't there more of there than here?'
Crab Apple Jelly

9. Father Ring was a plausible little Kerryman with a sand-coloured puss and a shock of red hair. He was always very deprecating, with an excuse-me air, and he came in sideways, on tiptoe, with a shocked expression – it is only Kerrymen who can do things like that.
Crab Apple Jelly

1. Anyone that got money out of a priest ought to have a statue put up to them.
Crab Apple Jelly

2. 'There are two classes of people, Charliss – those who gravitate towards the poorhouse and those who gravitate towards the gaol.'
Crab Apple Jelly

3. 'Great God,' he fumed, when his wife was having her first baby, 'nine months over a little job like that! I'd do it in three if I could only get started.'
Crab Apple Jelly

4. At the age of eighteen to be told that there can be anything one doesn't know about love is like a knife in the heart.
Crab Apple Jelly

5. He was a proud man and a high-principled one, though what his principles were based on was more than I ever discovered.
An Only Child

6. Father had a secret of making inanimate objects appear to possess malevolent life of their own, and sometimes it was hard to believe that his tools and materials were not really in a conspiracy against him.
An Only Child

7. She had only two faults that I ever knew of – she was vain and she was obstinate – and the fact that these qualities were masked by humility and gentleness prevented my recognising them till I was a grown man.
An Only Child

8. Mother realised, to her great astonishment, that Betty was a Protestant as well. Nobody had ever explained to her that Protestants could also be poor.
An Only Child

9. She never went to bed at all because in her early years she had seen someone die in bed, and never cared for beds after. When she died herself, she was sitting bolt upright in the chair where she had slept for twenty years.
An Only Child

10. So I adored education from afar, and strove to be worthy of it, as later I adored beautiful girls and strove to be worthy of them, and with similar results.
An Only Child

11. He combined the sanctimoniousness of a reformed pirate with the brutality of a half-witted drill sergeant. With him the cane was never a mere weapon; it was a real extension of his personality, like a musicians's instrument or a ventriloquist's dummy.
An Only Child

1. Never having anyone to teach me, I learned only by pretending to know.
An Only Child

2. I got my first job through my confessor, a gentle old priest who regarded me as a very saintly boy, and regularly asked me to pray for his intention. If innocence and sanctity are related, he was probably not far wrong about me because once I confessed to 'bad thoughts', meaning, I suppose, murdering my grandmother, but Father O'Regan interpreted it differently, and there ensued an agonising few minutes in which he asked me questions I didn't understand, and I gave him answers that he didn't understand, and I suspect that when I left the confession box, the poor man was as shaken as I was.
An Only Child

3. Indeed it would be truer to say that the Irish nation and myself were both engaged in an elaborate process of improvisation. I was improvising an education I could not afford, and the country was improvising a revolution it could not afford.
An Only Child

4. Irish teachers, like American policemen, never having learned that to go about armed is not the best way of securing obedience and respect.
An Only Child

Joe
O'Connor

5. You can't help feeling that if the Éamon de Valera generation had stayed home and changed the occasional nappy, Ireland might well have been better off.
The Sunday Tribune, April 1994

Peadar
O'Donnell

6. 'There's people in this island, an' the heaviest of their work is puttin' out rumours.'
Islanders

7. 'Wasn't he the greatest oarsmen in the island in his day?' Charlie asked.
   'He was, but his day went down early.'
Islanders

Sean
O'Faolain

8. If there is one British thing the Irish have always learned to fear, and with good reason, it is British diplomacy.
The Life Story of Éamon de Valera

9. Love is like jungle warfare at night, it keys you up, you feel things you can't see.
The Heat of the Sun

1. When we couldn't marry you were so afraid to lose me that you never uttered a word about religion, and now, when we can marry, you give the choice of being a cad if I don't and a Catholic if I do.
The Heat of the Sun

2. There are so few sins, and they repeat themselves endlessly. Even boringly. It is only the circumstances that change.
The Heat of the Sun

3. A false-brogue, as every Irishman knows, is a sure sign that the speaker is about to say something so true that he wants to blunt the edge of it by presenting it as a kind of family joke.
The Heat of the Sun

4. They say there's nothing like a good grouse for a bad theologian.
The Heat of the Sun

5. He had the smouldering ill-disposed eyes of the incorrigible Celt – 'always eager to take offence', as the fourth member of the party had already cracked.
Selected Stories

6. Did it ever occur to you that the bottom of a whiskey bottle is much too near the top?
Selected Stories

7. Cows to her had always meant only two white bottles tinkling on her front step in Saint Rita's Villas.
The Talking Trees

8. They dreamed of clouds upon clouds of fat, pink, soft, ardent girls billowing towards them across the horizon of their future. They might just as well have been dreaming of pink porpoises moaning at their feet for love.
The Talking Trees

9. Always near every school, there is a Daisy Boister – the fast girl whom everybody has heard about and nobody knows.
The Talking Trees

10. 'I hope to God,' Jimmy said, 'he has our pound note. I don't know in hell why you made that slob our treasurer.'
    'Because he is poor,' Dick said quietly. 'We would have spent it.'
The Talking Trees

11. One look at him, a couple of questions, and any stranger would have had it all. He looked about forty-five (he was thirty-six); his hair was grey as a badger; his lower eyelids were as pink as a bloodhound's; his trousers gave him legs like an elephant; he walked like a seal; and he had been on the booze for some fifteen years.
The Talking Trees

12. Few things are more dear to the heart of a peasant than a clean pedigree. It keeps history at bay.
The Talking Trees

13. They were the most supremely splendid, perfect,

godawful examples of bad art I had ever seen. As I gazed at them in a Cortes silence I knew that I simply must possess one of them immediately.
The Talking Trees

1. He might have ranked with the best of Dublin's legendary monologuists. He lacked their professional self-assurance. However carefully guffers like Wilde, Shaw, Stephens, Yeats or Gogarty prepared their *dits* they always threw them away, assured that there would be an infielder to catch them, an audience to applaud.
Foreign Affairs

2. Familiarity breeds envy, and that conspiracy, and that skulduggery.
Foreign Affairs

3. Twice on the way to the front door he paused, as if to admire the grounds, really to assure himself that no dog had failed to read the NO DOGS sign: a born cityman, he feared all living animals. He was very fond of them in poetry.
Foreign Affairs

4. 'Passion!' he amended. 'For this agony there are only three solutions. The first is sin, which,' he grinned, 'I am informed on the best authority is highly agreeable but involves an awful waste of time. I mean if you could hang a girl up in the closet every time you were finished with her that would be very convenient, but. Then there is marriage, which as Shaw said is the perfect combination of maximum temptation and maximum opportunity. And there is celibacy of which, I can say with authority, as the only member of the present company who knows anything at all about it, that it bestows on man the qualified freedom of a besieged city where one sometimes has to eat rats.
Foreign Affairs

Liam
O'Flaherty

5. He was interested in art, literature, politics, sociology, history and every new direction of human thought. But his mind seemed to have no faculty for measuring the relative values of any two ideas, discoveries or facts; so that a brown mole on a peasant's left ear was as important and interesting to him as the discovery of radium, the Russian Revolution or the crucifixion of Jesus Christ.
The Wilderness

6. The young men of the neighbourhood had gathered in Mrs Dillon's cottage. Although none of them was aware of it, they had all come in pursuit of Mrs Dillon. She was the only attractive young woman in that part of the glen; and being

married to a degenerate husband who maintained her in dire poverty, her restless soul vented its spleen on society by arousing the passions of all the males in her environment.
The Wilderness

Criostoir
O'Flynn

1. Metaphors, said Bobby, are popularly considered to be things that flash across the night sky in November.
Sanctuary Island

2. You said we're never angry with anybody now since the English gave up trying to civilise us, only with the neighbouring parish when and if they conquer us in the national sport of hurling . . . the blood-and-bandages game you called it.
Sanctuary Island

3. In the early years of his manhood, Clancy, like most of his fellows, sought relief from the toil of the day in the pub and the bookie's. Until the voracious mouths in the nest became so many that Clancy could only visit the pub at Christmas, and the bookie on nightmares.
Sanctuary Island

4. Whole country is rotten with ruins. Kind of a shock to see Shannon Airport so shiny bright and new. Almost expect a round tower there too.
Sanctuary Island

5. Goddam officials and their laws, always making a nuisance for somebody. Didn't the Almighty make the commandments long ago, and he only made ten.
Sanctuary Island

6. The official Irish title of the police force was *An Garda Síochána*, the Guardians of the Peace; the unfortunate thing about Shamus's two years in this town was that it had become all monotonous *síochán* and no call at all for the Garda.
Sanctuary Island

Brendan
Ó hEithir

7. The [censorship] legislation was intended to keep the Irish people pure in mind and tranquil in the most sensitive areas of their anatomy. In short, it was all about Ireland's great preoccupation: the illicit 'dart of the other thing', or sex as it is known in the civilised world.
Begrudger's Guide to Irish Politics

8. Mr de Valera, like Mr Cosgrave, regarded literary censorship as part of our freedom to achieve fuller freedom.
Begrudger's Guide to Irish Politics

1. What has been noticed, and not only by begrudgers, but by every justice and judge sufficiently sober to be aware of what is going on in his court, is that there seems to be no respect at all for the oath in Ireland, and that this has been the case for years. They are swallowed daily, and not just by plaintiffs, defendants and witnesses but by members of the Garda Síochána as well, as if they were raw eggs and sherry.
Begrudger's Guide to Irish Politics

2. [de Valera] brought over Pierpoint to hang Maurice O'Neill and Charlie Kerins. Republicans said that at least Blythe would have attempted to find a hangman who would be able to ask the victim in Irish if the knot was tickling his ear.
Begrudger's Guide to Irish Politics

3. Clann na Talún was unique among Irish political parties to gain representation in Dáil Éireann by having almost no policies apart from remedying farmers' grievances: a task beyond human, or even divine, competence.
Begrudger's Guide to Irish Politics

4. Lenin said that one of his missions in life was to abolish the village idiot. It is just as well, for the sake of many of our pillars of rural democracy, that Comrade Lenin's writ never ran in Ireland.
Begrudger's Guide to Irish Politics

5. Alas, poor Lynch! The weather and the times should really have kept in tune with his rosy, sweetly scented vision of the Ireland of crushed grass, mature Paddy and 'the wicked chuckle of hurleys' in the Tipperary square: the Ireland where the safe period meant the teams and the crowd standing to attention and facing the flag for the national anthem.
Begrudger's Guide to Irish Politics

Kevin O'Higgins

6. [In 1918] O'Higgins was arrested and charged with the offence that 'he did unlawfully assemble and . . . disturb the peace . . .' After a week in Mountjoy prison, . . . he was brought . . . in a heavily guarded train to Tullamore for trial. He defended himself vigorously and was unsparing of the two policemen who were state witnesses, inquiring of the sergeant who gave evidence 'whether he had ever committed perjury before?' And when the sergeant admitted that he had not taken down [O'Higgins'] speech but had made 'mental notes', O'Higgins replied: 'I suggest that

you had a good deal of blank
space for that purpose.'
in *Kevin O'Higgins* by Terence de
Vere White

Arthur
O'Neill

1. From that to Moneymore,
which I might then justly call
Moneyless, as I was uncommonly
bare of money.
Autobiography

2. I made off for the County
Tyrone again, and notwith-
standing my being blind and of
course being incapacitated from
being useful either in loyalty or
treason, I had to get a pass; and
without considering my
incapacity the wiseacres on my
way home demanded my pass
almost every five minutes. I
would sometimes say 'here it is',
pointing to my harp; and because
there was no crown on it I was
often in danger of being ill-used
by the illiterate loyalists, who
took pride in displaying their
cautious conduct.
Autobiography

T. F.
O'Rahilly

3. Ni i geomhnuidhe mharbhann
daidín fia.
(It is not every day daddy kills a
deer.)
A Miscellany of Irish Proverbs

4. Cheithre nithe nách tugtha
d'Éireannaach ionntaoibh léo, ii.
adharc bhó, crúb chapaill, dranna
madra, agus gáire Sagsanaigh.
(Four things which an Irishman
ought not to trust – a cow's horn,
a horse's hoof, a dog's snarl and
an Englishman's laugh.)
A Miscellany of Irish Proverbs

Ian
Paisley

5. The Catholics have been
interfering in Ulster affairs since
1641.
The Irish Times, August 1968

6. He is talking to a God Who is
greater than Mr Ted Heath or Mr
Willie Whitelaw, Hallelujah! He is
talking to a God Who is greater
than Sean MacStiofain and David
O'Connell.
*The Dagger of Treachery Strikes
at the Heart of Ulster*

7. When I am told I say a terrible
thing, I always like to repeat it. It
is always worthy of repetition.
*The Dagger of Treachery Strikes
at the Heart of Ulster*

8. Some of them are thinking of a
united Ireland with John Hume
as king, Bernadette Devlin as
queen and Gerry Fitt as the court
jester.
*The Dagger of Treachery Strikes
at the Heart of Ulster*

9. I made a vow that no one
would ever slam a door on me

again. So when I went to the next house I put my big foot through the door and many a person struggled to close the door, but that foot kept it open and many a time I preached through the little slot as they attempted to close the door.
The Four Windows of Life

1. Of course, I am a nobody and a nothing, and everybody will tell you that. They will say that I'm only an upstart. Glorious upstart for the Lord!
The Four Windows of Life

2. So I was thrown, in my early ministry, into the Protestant controversy. I have never regretted that and never will, for from my head to my toe I am a Protestant, and if there is any dirt under the toenails it is Protestant dirt.
The Four Windows of Life

Hyacinth *Plunkett*

3. 'There is a very unpleasant smell in this Court,' he said. 'O yes, my Lord,' said Hycie, 'we noticed it even before your Lordship came in.'
in *The Old Munster Circuit* by Maurice Healy

4. 'D'ye think I'd stoop so far as to dine with a couple of Removable Magistrates?' 'O-o-o-o!' shrilled

Hycie, with an apologetic gesture of his hands, 'just to punish them, Mattie; just to punish them!'
in *The Old Munster Circuit* by Maurice Healy

James *Plunkett*

5. 'I heard tell of a raffle someone ran once,' Hennessy explained. 'The first prize was a week's holiday in Belfast. And do you know what the second prize was?'
    He paused long enough to fix their attention. Then he said:
    'The second prize was two weeks' holiday in Belfast.'
Strumpet City

6. 'It's all sanctified ground.'
    'Not the boiler house,' Hennessy argued. 'Sanctifying the boiler house would be a bit Irish. You might as well say the toilet at the back of the vestry was sanctified.'
Strumpet City

7. 'It amused me to see our principal street dedicated so entirely to love.'
    Father O'Connor's pale eyebrows shot up.
    'Parnell at the top – an adulterer,' Yearling explained. 'Nelson in the middle – another adulterer. And at the end O'Connell – a notorious wencher.'
Strumpet City

1. 'That's the difference between the amateur and the professional. The amateur has to have his music – but the professional plays by ear. Supposing, every time I went to play at a race-meeting, I had to stick a music stand up in front of me, what'd happen?'
Strumpet City

2. 'Jeremiah had three faults that made him a bad publican,' Rashers said. 'He stocked only the best, he kept too easy a slate and his best customer was himself.'
Strumpet City

Sarah Purser

3. Sarah Purser, or some other witty woman in Dublin, said about George Moore: 'Gentlemen kiss and never tell. Cads kiss and tell. George doesn't kiss but he tells.'
in *Irish Literary Portraits* by W. R. Rodgers

George Roberts

4. [Of James Joyce] [He] circulated a letter to all his friends – and some of his enemies – requesting money to raise the fare. In the letter I received, the fare was multiplied by two, he wasn't travelling alone. To free Dublin from his presence seemed very cheap at the price, so most of us heartily subscribed.
in *Irish Literary Portraits* by W. R. Rodgers

Nicholas Robinson

5. Friends are like fiddle-strings – they must not be screwed too much.
The Irish Times, April 1993

Sir Boyle Roche

6. Last Thurday an alarm was given that a gang of rebels, in full retreat from Drogheda, were advancing under the French standard; but they had no colours, nor any drums except bagpipes.
Letter

7. We put them all to the sword; not a soul of them escaped alive except some that were drowned in the adjoining bog.
Letter

8. The only living beasts on the farms of Ireland are the birds that fly over them.
in *The Book of Irish Bull* by Des MacHale

9. The cup of Ireland's miseries has been overflowing for centuries, but it is not yet full.
in *The Book of Irish Bull* by Des MacHale

10. Many hundreds of people were destitute even of the very goods they possess.
in *The Book of Irish Bull* by Des MacHale

1. Iron gates will last forever and afterwards they can be used for making horse shoes.
in *The Book of Irish Bull* by Des MacHale

2. By trial by jury I have lived, and please God with trial by jury I shall die.
in *The Book of Irish Bull* by Des MacHale

3. Three-quarters of what the opposition says about us is lies and the other half is without any foundation in truth.
in *The Book of Irish Bull* by Des MacHale

4. The man who would stoop so low as to write an anonymous letter, the least he might do is to sign his name to it.
in *The Book of Irish Bull* by Des MacHale

5. Mister Speaker, the country is in such a desperate state that little children, who can neither walk nor talk, are running around the street cursing their maker.
in *The Book of Irish Bull* by Des MacHale

6. I answer in the affirmative with an emphatic 'No!'
in *The Book of Irish Bull* by Des MacHale

7. I would give up half – nay, the whole of the constitution to preserve the remainder.
in *The Book of Irish Bull* by Des MacHale

8. Why should we do anything for posterity, what has posterity ever done for us? . . . By posterity, gentlemen, I do not mean our ancestors, but those who came immediately after them.
in *The Book of Irish Bull* by Des MacHale

9. Single misfortunes rarely come alone and the worst of all misfortunes is usually followed by a greater misfortune.
in *The Book of Irish Bull* by Des MacHale

10. The only way of preventing what is past is to put a stop to it before it happens.
in *The Book of Irish Bull* by Des MacHale

11. No man can be in two places at the one time, unless he is a bird.
in *The Book of Irish Bull* by Des MacHale

12. [On Northern Protestants] A disorderly set of people whom no king can govern and no God can please.
in *Theobald Wolfe Tone* by Henry Boylan

W. R. Rodgers

13. The truth is that the Irish are too fond of the spoken word to bother overmuch about the written word.
Irish Literary Portraits

1. [Of J. M. Synge's mother] She was one of those downright, upright, Northern breed which loved a good floury potato and a good flowery sermon.
Irish Literary Portraits

2. [Of G.B. Shaw] Some men are born great, and some are more grating than others.
Irish Literary Portraits

3. [Of G.B. Shaw] Every skeleton has a human being in the cupboard.
Irish Literary Portraits

Bill
Rolston

4. Their argument is that Cu Chulainn was the first UDA man.
The Irish Times, January 1993

Amanda McKittrick
Ros

5. For every finger of his filthy hands, every toe of his treacherous feet, he as often had robbed the dainty daughters of distinction, the elegant heiresses of wealth untold, the brunettes of brother dignities, the pretending daughters of saintly divines, down to the most modest maids-of-all-words, priceless pearls neither money nor prayers could ever reset.
Helen Huddleson

6. Delina imagined an air of great Christian charity encompassed hospitals. She found a wide gulf separated their hallowed midst from the hall of satanic evil in which she was obliged to stay for a period of six months.
Delina Delany

7. Delina was unable to cast from her the weight of apprehension that dragged so heavily on her young heart. She had not been taught at the school of female art that involved in its craft the knack of wearing a face of joy where sorrow was its soul foundation, and hiding it in pleasant smiles.
Delina Delany

William
Ross

8. The Roman Catholic community has always been wider apart between their left and their right elements than the Protestant/Unionist community, and they have never really managed to bridge that.
The Irish Times, April 1994

George (AE)
Russell

9. Graves should be but for the dead,
Not for things that still have breath.

What could use the living so?
Time, more murderous than
    death.

Time has buried love alive
In the heart, and day by day
O'er the pious image casts
Shovelfuls of airy clay.
Collected Poems

1. A myriad loves
Her heart would confess,
That thought but one
To be wantonness.
Collected Poems

2. So thronged was her spirit
It seemed a pack
That carried the moon
And stars on her back.
Collected Poems

3. A good many years ago you
grafted a slip of poetry on your
economic tree. I do not know if
you expected a hybrid.
The National Being

4. What too many people in
Ireland mistake for thoughts is
feelings.
The National Being

5. Nations which form their ideas
and marry them in the hurry of
passion are likely to repent
without leisure and they will not
be able to divorce these ideas
without prolonged domestic
squabbles and public cleansing of
dirty linen.
The National Being

6. Men who love Ireland ignobly
brawl about her in their cups,
quarrel about her with their
neighbours, allow no freedom of
thought of her or service of her
other than their own, take to the
cudgel and the rifle, and join
sectarian orders or lodges to
ensure that Ireland will be made
in their ignoble image.
The National Being

7. A literary movement consists of
half a dozen writers living in the
same city who cordially detest
one another.
in *Irish Literary Portraits* by
W. R. Rodgers

George Bernard
Shaw

8. As a matter of fact, the sound
of English makes me feel at
home; and I dislike feeling at
home when I am abroad. It is not
precisely what one goes to the
expense for.
Widowers' Houses

9. Advanced people form
charming friendships:
conventional people marry.
The Philanderer

10. When two ladies quarrel in
this club, it is against the rules to
settle it when there are
gentlemen present: especially the
gentlemen they are quarrelling
about.
The Philanderer

1. There are no secrets better kept than the secrets everybody guesses.
Mrs Warren's Profession

2. I'm not a fool in the ordinary sense: only in the Scriptural sense of doing all the things the wise man declared to be folly, after trying them himself on the most extensive scale.
Mrs Warren's Profession

3. What use are cartridges in battle? I always carry chocolate instead.
Arms and the Man

4. I don't mind a good wash once a week to keep up my position; but once a day is carrying the thing to a ridiculous extreme.
Arms and the Man

5. My rank is the highest known in Switzerland: I am a free citizen.
Arms and the Man

6. The overpaying instinct is a generous one: better than the underpaying instinct, and not so common.
Candida

7. I'm only a beer teetotaller, not a champagne teetotaller. I don't like beer.
Candida

8. We innkeepers have plenty of cheap wine: we think nothing of spilling it. You great generals have plenty of cheap blood: you think nothing of spilling it.
The Man of Destiny

9. Though I am a married woman, I have never been in love; I have never had a love affair; and, to be quite frank with you, Mr Valentine, what I have seen of the love affairs of other people has not led me to regret that deficiency in my experience.
You Never Can Tell

10. A man's power of love and admiration is like any other of his powers: he has to throw it away many times before he learns what is really worthy of it.
You Never Can Tell

11. We do unkind things in a kind way: we say bitter things in a sweet voice: we always give our friends chloroform when we tear them to pieces.
You Never Can Tell

12. The British soldier can stand up to anything except the British War Office.
The Devil's Disciple

13. When a stupid man is doing something he is ashamed of, he always declares that it is his duty.
Caesar and Cleopatra

14. The more things a man is ashamed of, the more respectable he is.
Man and Superman

1. It is the self-sacrificing women that sacrifice others most recklessly.
Man and Superman

2. A broken heart is a very pleasant complaint for a man in London if he has a comfortable income.
Man and Superman

3. Beauty is all very well at first sight; but who ever looks at it when it has been in the house three days?
Man and Superman

4. There are two tragedies in life. One is to lose your heart's desire. The other is to gain it.
Man and Superman

5. Dhrink is the curse of me unhappy counthry. I take it meself because I've a wake heart and a poor digestion; but in principle I'm a teetoatler.
John Bull's Other Island

6. An Irishman's heart is nothing but his imagination.
John Bull's Other Island

7. There are great possibilities for Ireland. Home Rule will work wonders under English guidance.
John Bull's Other Island

8. Live in contact with dreams and you will get something of their charm: live in contact with facts and you will get something of their brutality.
John Bull's Other Island

9. The more a man knows, and the farther he travels, the more likely he is to marry a country girl afterwards.
John Bull's Other Island

10. I see no evils in the world – except, of course, natural evils – that cannot be remedied by freedom, self-government, and English institutions. I think so, not because I am an Englishman, but as a matter of common sense.
John Bull's Other Island

11. I know I have a strong sense of humour which sometimes makes people doubt whether I am quite serious.
John Bull's Other Island

12. First love is only a little foolishness and a lot of curiosity.
John Bull's Other Island

13. What really flatters a man is that you think him worth flattering.
John Bull's Other Island

14. He broke the law when he was born: his parents were not married.
Major Barbara

15. It is only in the middle classes, Stephen, that people get into a state of dumb helpless horror when they find that there are wicked people in the world.
Major Barbara

16. Greek scholars are privileged men. Few of them know Greek;

and none of them know anything else; but their position is unchallengable. Other languages are the qualifications of waiters and commercial travellers.
Major Barbara

1. UNDERSHAFT: Alcohol is a very necessary article. It heals the sick.
BARBARA: It does nothing of the sort.
UNDERSHAFT: Well, it assists the doctor: that is perhaps a less questionable way of putting it.
Major Barbara

2. Every true Englishman detests the English.
Major Barbara

3. Most discoveries are made regularly every fifteen years.
The Doctor's Dilemma

4. All professions are conspiracies against the laity.
The Doctor's Dilemma

5. I must say you Gentiles are very hard to please. You say we are no gentlemen when we lend you money; and when we refuse to lend it you say just the same.
The Doctor's Dilemma

6. When I was only a company officer I had at least the right to expose myself to death in the field. Now I'm a General even that resource is cut off.
Getting married

7. If I am to be a mother, I really cannot have a man bothering me to be a wife at the same time.
Getting married

8. A man is like a phonograph with half-a-dozen records. You soon get tired of them all; and yet you have to sit at table whilst he reels them off to every new visitor.
Getting married

9. Marriage is good enough for the lower classes; they have facilities for desertion that are denied to us.
Getting married

10. Who am I that I should rebuke you? Besides, I know there are discussions in which the poker is the only possible argument.
Getting married

11. The Sheriff knows the law. I wouldn't say for sure; but I think it would be more seemly to have a witness. Go and round one up.
The Shewing-up of Blanco Posnet

12. The man that is not prejudiced against a horse-thief is not fit to sit on a jury in this town.
The Shewing-up of Blanco Posnet

13. If I started being ashamed of myself I shouldn't have time for anything else.
Misalliance

1. All Shaw's characters are himself: mere puppets stuck up to spout Shaw.
Fanny's First Play

2. I like wanting you. As long as I have a want, I have a reason for living. Satisfaction is death.
Overruled

3. Danger is delicious. But death isn't. We court the danger; but the real delight is in escaping, after all.
Overruled

4. All the volcanic women I know are plain little creatures with sandy hair.
Overruled

5. Time enough to think of the future when you haven't any future to think of.
Pygmalion

6. Undeserving poverty is my line.
Pygmalion

7. I sold flowers. I didn't sell myself. Now you've made a lady of me I'm not fit to sell anything else.
Pygmalion

8. The difference between a lady and a flower girl is not how she behaves, but how she's treated.
Pygmalion

9. Would the world ever have been made if its maker had been afraid of making trouble? Making life means making trouble.
Pygmalion

10. ELLIE: But how can you love a liar?
MRS HUSHABYE: I don't know. But you can, fortunately. Otherwise there wouldn't be much love in the world.
Heartbreak House

11. Quite a lot of women have flirted with me because I am quite safe; but they get tired of me for the same reason.
Heartbreak House

12. The important thing is not to have the last word, but to have your own way.
Heartbreak House

13. ELLIE: Why do women always want other women's husbands?
CAPTAIN SHOTOVER: Why do horse-thieves prefer a horse that is broken-in to one that is wild?
Heartbreak House

14. It's prudent to gain the whole world and lose your own soul. But don't forget that your soul sticks to you if you stick to it; but the world has a way of slipping through your fingers.
Heartbreak House

15. Every drunken skipper trusts to Providence. But one of the ways of Providence with drunken skippers is to run them on the rocks.
Heartbreak House

1. I don't know about it's being a great war, sir. It's a big war; but that's not the same thing.
O'Flaherty V. C.

2. Do you think we should have got an army without conscription if domestic life had been as happy as people say it is?
O'Flaherty V. C.

3. Things wear out by practice: they do not grow by it.
Back to Methuselah

4. It's only the politicians who improve the world so gradually that nobody can see the improvement.
Back to Methusaleh

5. You have at last become prudent: you are no longer what you call a sportsman: you are a sensible coward, almost a grown-up man.
Back to Methusaleh

6. Decency cannot be discussed without indecency.
Back to Methusaleh

7. We want a few mad people now. See where the sane ones have landed us!
Saint Joan

8. Our soldiers are always beaten because they are fighting only to save their skins; and the shortest way to save your skin is to run away.
Saint Joan

9. Minding your own business is like minding your own body; it's the shortest way to make yourself sick.
Saint Joan

10. The Jews generally give value. They make you pay; but they deliver the goods. In my experience the men who want something for nothing are invariably Christians.
Saint Joan

11. I can keep to the point – when it suits me. And I can keep you to the point, sir, whether it suits you or not.
The Apple Cart

12. The best speech in the world can be read in such a way as to set the audience laughing at it.
The Apple Cart

13. Nothing annoys a man more than a woman who talks to him about his business and pretends to understand it.
Jitta's Atonement

14. The theory of legal procedure is that if you set two liars to expose one another the truth will emerge.
Too True to be Good

15. What is the use of leading the House if it never goes anywhere.
On the Rocks

1. Sermons and speeches are not religion, not patriotism, not politics: they are only the gibberings of ghosts from the past.
On the Rocks

2. We were commanded to love our enemies because loving is good for us and dreadfully bad for them.
The Simpleton of the Unexpected Isles

3. I never utter a libel. My father instructed me most carefully in the law of libel. If I questioned your solvency, that would be a libel. If I suggested that you are unfaithful to your wife, that would be a libel. But if I call you a rhinoceros – which you are: a most unmitigated rhinoceros – that is only vulgar abuse.
The Millionairess

4. My dear father used to say that in the law courts there is only one way to beat the people who have unlimited money; and that is to have no money at all.
The Millionairess

5. Motor oil is a sanction when you withhold it. Castor oil is a sanction when you administer it.
Geneva

6. I am sick of reasonable people: they see all the reasons for being lazy and doing nothing.
Geneva

7. I greatly mistrust advanced people. In my experience they are very difficult to work with, and often most disreputable in their private lives.
Geneva

8. NELL: It is not fair of her to keep mentioning my profession when I cannot decently mention hers.
'In Good King Charles's Golden Days'

9. They made me a prefect and gave me a cane to beat the boys they were too lazy to beat themselves. That was what they called teaching me leadership.
Buoyant Billions

10. I am never happy. I don't want to be happy. I want to be alive and active. Bothering about happiness is the worst unhappiness.
Buoyant Billions

J. D.
Sheridan

11. The money I give to the carol-singers is no better than blackmail; I want to get it over quickly and get back to my typing; I pay the piper but I never listen to the tune.
Funnily Enough

12. An Irishman speaks of 'my wife' only on very formal occasions or when he is explaining why he is loitering in

the vestibule of a ladies' hair-dressing salon. At all other times he speaks of 'the wife', and uses the definite article because he is speaking of a very definite article. He has no need, as a man might in Reno or Los Angeles, to be more precise, and he can make his meaning clear without specifying whether he is referring to the current edition or to a back number.
Funnily Enough

1. Whether a man follows the sea or the plough, his gait gives him away, and it is not for nothing that people speak of a 'walk of life'.
Funnily Enough

2. The first rule of visitor-hospitality is that the visitor must never get a glimpse of the conditions in which you normally live.
My Hat Blew Off

3. Most murder stories, I notice, begin with a house party, and writers of detective fiction make a great bother about motive and opportunity. But there are motives and motives, and if I am ever called in to solve a house-party murder I shall concentrate my attention on the host. And instead of asking why he killed one of the guests I shall ask him why he let the rest of them go on living.
My Hat Blew Off

4. It has been said about him that he would play Poker anywhere and at any time, but this is a cruel exaggeration – he wouldn't play in the front seat of the chapel on the last night of the men's mission.
My Hat Blew Off

5. A man cuts the back garden only when he has to choose between cutting it and letting the shooting rights.
My Hat Blew Off

6. A garden is a nuisance, or a lovesome thing, according to how you look at it. But it gets you in the end. For there is no getting away from grass. Whether you grudge the time you spend cutting it, or welcome it for the social amenities that go with it, you may be reasonably sure that something very like it will grow over your grave.
My Hat Blew Off

7. The world is full of people who think that a man who doesn't beat his wife or steal pennies from blind men must be fond of dogs – though there is just as much reason for believing that he must be fond of marsh-mallows.
My Hat Blew Off

Margaret Burke
Sheridan

8. [To a rival singer] My dear, you're just a Woolworths' soprano.

Richard Brinsley
Sheridan

1. There is nothing on earth so easy as to forget, if a person chooses to set about it.
The Rivals

2. 'Tis safest in matrimony to begin with a little aversion.
The Rivals

3. A circulating library in a town is as an evergreen tree of diabolical knowledge!
The Rivals

4. A lie is nothing unless one supports it. Sir, whenever I draw on my invention for a good current lie, I always forge endorsements as well as the bill.
The Rivals

5. Though I never scruple a lie to serve my master, yet it hurts one's conscience to be found out.
The Rivals

6. There is no meaning in the common oaths, and nothing but their antiquity makes them respectable.
The Rivals

7. I am so poor, that I can't afford to do a dirty action.
The Rivals

8. I should rather choose a wife of mine to have the usual number of limbs and a limited quantity of back: and thought one eye may be very agreeable, yet as the prejudice has always run in favour of two, I would not wish to affect a singularity in that article.
The Rivals

9. MRS MALAPROP: It gives me the hydrostatics to such a degree – I thought she had persisted from corresponding with him; but, behold, this very day I have interceded another letter from the fellow.
The Rivals

10. The quarrel is a very pretty quarrel as it stands; we should only spoil it by trying to explain it.
The Rivals

11. If I can't get a wife without fighting for her, by my valour! I'll live a bachelor.
The Rivals

12. Rum agreed with her well enough; it was not the rum that killed the poor dear creature, for she died of a dropsy.
St Patrick's Day

13. He would have deceived a chief justice: the dog seemed as ignorant as my clerk, and talked of honesty as if he had been a churchwarden.
St Patrick's Day

14. DOCTOR ROSY: I'll certainly see justice done on your murderer.

JUSTICE CREDULOUS: I thank you, my dear friend, but I had rather see it myself.
St Patrick's Day

1. He left his old religion for an estate, and has not had time to get a new one.
The Duenna

2. Like an unskilled gunner he usually misses his aim and is hurt by the recoil of his own piece.
The Duenna

3. We never expected any love from one another, and so we were never disappointed. If we grumbled a little now and then, it was soon over, for we were never fond enough to quarrel.
The Duenna

4. At twenty she mocks at the duty you taught her –
Oh, what a plague is an obstinate daughter!
The Duenna

5. Those Dutch and English traders, as you call them, are the wiser people. Why, booby, in England they were formerly as nice, as to birth and family, as we are: but they have long since discovered what a wonderful purifier gold is; and now no one there regards pedigree in anything but a horse.
The Duenna

6. A bumper of good liquor
Will end a contest quicker
Than justice, judge, or vicar.
The Duenna

7. Conscience has more to do with gallantry than it has with politics.
The Duenna

8. I am the worst company in the world at a concert, I'm so apt to attend to the music.
A Trip to Scarborough

9. Suspense is at all times the devil, but of all modes of suspense, the watching for a loitering mistress is the worst.
A Trip to Scarborough

10. To say truth, ma'am, 'tis very vulgar to print; and, as my little productions are mostly satires and lampoons on particular people, I find they circulate more by giving copies in confidence to friends of the parties.
The School for Scandal

11. If you wanted authority over me, you should have adopted me, and not married me; I am sure you were old enough.
The School for Scandal

12. After having married you, I should never pretend to taste again.
The School for Scandal

13. Come, come, 'tis not that she paints so ill – but, when she has finished her face, she joins it so

badly to her neck, that she looks like a mended statue, in which the connoisseur may see at once that the head's modern, though the trunk's antique!
The School for Scandal

1. When a scandalous story is believed against one, there certainly is no comfort like the consciousness of having deserved it.
The School for Scandal

2. I beg your ladyship ten thousand pardons: you paid me extremely liberally for the lie in question; but I unfortunately have been offered double to speak the truth.
The School for Scandal

3. I live by the badness of my character; and, if it were once known that I had been betrayed into an honest action, I should lose every friend I have in the world.
The School for Scandal

4. The theatre, in proper hands, might certainly be made the school of morality; but now, I am sorry to say it, people seem to go there principally for their entertainment!
The Critic

5. Can there on this earth be fools who seek for happiness, and pass by love in the pursuit?
Pizarro

Paul
Smith

6. But in Ireland inequalities did not vanish before the determined will.
Come Trailing Blood

7. Christina was thirty, and in the laundry where she worked, and in the house, and around the canal, people said, 'There's no flies on Christina Swords,' which meant she was more sensible than she, an unmarried woman her age, had any right to be.
Come Trailing Blood

8. It was all very well for the priests and their prayers to go on about forgiving those who trespassed against us. The priests like the rich were insured in heaven against the calamities.
Come Trailing Blood

9. A primitive, pagan and thriftless pack the Romans were when you got down to it – and that outburst from Mollo Goss, just another manifestation of their heathen worship of false idols to which they attributed all kinds of rigmaroles, invented by crafty Jesuits to keep in the depths of ignorance an island of backward peasants. Sophia munched and on her face hairs stirred as she thanked the Lord for her Presbyterian ancestors.
Come Trailing Blood

1. It is about time the British
government and people were
made to understand that poverty,
exploitation, ignorance and
oppression are not after all
conditions which nations can
endure.
Come Trailing Blood

R. M. (Bertie)
Smyllie

2. Smyllie's deputy, Alec
Newman, a man in his early
thirties, with a lot of very large
teeth, not much hair, and
wearing a pair of glasses as thick
as two slices of bread, is seated
at the desk immediately facing
the door.
'Good evening, Mr Smyllie,
sir,' he says with exaggerated
formality. 'All goes well with
you?'
'Bollocks, Mr Newman, sir,'
Smyllie replies affably. 'As you
well know, we are all in
desparate disarray.'
in *Mr Smyllie, Sir* by Tony Gray

3. 'It has always seemed to me,
Mr Gray, sir,' he remarked to me
one night around about that
time, 'that the best newspapers
are always run by a committee.
A commitee of one. The Editor.
In this particular case, my good
self.'
in *Mr Smyllie, Sir* by Tony Gray

4. . . . after I had been only about
three weeks on the paper Smyllie
told me that I could now take
charge of the Book Page . . . 'It
entails no more, Mr Gray, sir,' he
had said to me, 'than keeping an
eye on the review copies as they
come in . . . If any books of
obvious local Irish interest
happen to come in, you must
always mention them to me
before handing them out, and any
leftovers are yours to dispose of,
on a cash basis, at Messrs Greene
& Company, the booksellers in
Clare Street, who will give you
precisely one third of the marked
price. That is one of the perks of
the position. The other is that you
will acquire the rather
grandiloquent title of Literary
Editor. Do not let it turn your
head, however, as it means
nothing, since I am in fact
Literary Editor just as I am News
Editor and Sports Editor and
Editor of everything else on this
shuddering newspaper.'
in *Mr Smyllie, Sir* by Tony Gray

5. After the appointment of a
Belfast correspondent called
Withers, Smyllie summoned me
into his office in great glee to
announce: 'Do you realise, Gray,
that we are now in a unique
position to break with impunity
one of the basic rules of syntax.
We now have a Northern Ireland
correspondent by the name of
Withers. And consequently, if for

any reason we fail to telephone the bugger, we are probably the only shuddering outfit in the entire world that can say, with complete grammatical rectitude, that our Withers is unrung.'
in *Mr Smyllie, Sir* by Tony Gray

1. As Fleming made his way into the office that night he heard the sound of distant singing. The tune was that of the Hymn to Joy from the last movement of the Beethoven Choral Symphony, and he could distinguish, away down the corridor, Smylllie's unmistakable rich baritone booming out the words:

Down the hall the butler
    wandered,
Bent on Sodomistic crime . . .

This was only one of the many variations Smyllie and Alec Newman had devised to fit the theme that has now become the official anthem of the European Community; from the first week I worked on *The Irish Times* until the present moment I can never hear that magnificent music without hearing, in my inner mind, Smyllie's stout baritone and Newman's slightly quavering tenor, intoning to the strains of the music:

And the chamber maid was
    pregnant
For the forty-second time,
Fo-or the forty,
Fo-or the forty,

FOR THE FORTY-SECOND
    TIME!
in *Mr Smyllie, Sir* by Tony Gray

2. . . . Seamus Kelly walked in and asked for a job. 'Do you happen to know anything about the theatre?' Smyllie enquired. Seamus replied that he had been a member of an amateur dramatic society once. 'Good,' said Smyllie. 'You can start tonight as drama critic.'
in *Mr Smyllie, Sir* by Tony Gray

3. A lifetime of experience on this newspaper has taught me that unsolicited contributions are, without any exceptions, worthless. The correct procedure for dealing with them is to ascertain whether a stamped addressed envelope has been enclosed.
If it has, you are at liberty to steam the stamp off and use it for your own personal correspondence; that is the particular perk attached to this task, as they say in business circles. The contributions themselves and all other correspondence should be disposed of as quickly as possible. Ideally, everything should be burnt. That is the only sure and certain way to avoid becoming involved in a troublesome and possibly interminable dialogue with the public.
in *Mr Smyllie, Sir* by Tony Gray

Somerville, E. and Ross, M.

1. My hostess, Mrs Jeremiah Donovan, was a handsome young woman, tall, fair and flushed, agonised with hospitality, shy to ferocity. The family dog was lifted from the hearth with a side kick worthy of an International football match; her offspring, clustered, staring, in the chimney-corner, were dispersed with a scorching whisper, of which the words, 'ye brazen tinkers', gave some clue to its general trend.
Some Experiences of an Irish R.M.

2. The next Petty Sessions day was wet; the tall windows of the Court House were grey and steaming, and the reek of wet humanity ascended to the ceiling. As I took my seat on the bench I perceived with an inward groan that the services of the two most eloquent solicitors in Skebawn had been engaged. This meant that Justice would not have run its course till heaven knew what dim hour of the afternoon, and that that course would be devious and difficult.
Some Experiences of an Irish R.M.

3. All the pews and galleries (any Irish court-house might, with the addition of a harmonium, pass presentably as a dissenting chapel) were full.
Some Experiences of an Irish R.M.

4. When I heard that Bernard Shute, of Clountiss, Esquire, late Lieutenant R.N., was running an Agricultural Show, to be held in his own demesne, I did not for a moment credit him with either philanthropy or public spirit. I recognised in it merely another outbreak of his exasperating health and energy. He bombarded the country with circulars, calling upon farmers for exhibits, and upon all for subscriptions; he made raids into neighbouring districts in his motor car, turning vague promises into bullion, with a success in mendicancy fortunately given to few. It was in a thoroughly ungenerous spirit that I yielded up my guinea and promised to attend the show in my thousands: peace at twenty-one shillings was comparatively cheap, and there was always a hope that it might end there.
Some Experiences of an Irish R.M.

5. It is impossible to imagine how we pursued an uninjured course through the companies of horsemen, the crowded carts, the squealing colts, the irresponsible led horses, and, most immutable of all obstacles, the groups of countrywomen, with the hoods of their cloaks over their heads.

They looked like nuns of some obscure order; they were deaf and blind as ramparts of sandbags; nothing less callous to human life than a Parisian cabdriver could have burst a way through them.
Some Experiences of an Irish R.M.

1. 'As a rule, I am so bored by driving that I find it reviving to be frightened.'
Some Experiences of an Irish R.M.

2. We sat there, and the moon and the round red Chinese lantern looked at each other across the evening, and had a certain resemblance, and I reflected on the fact that an Irishman is always a critic in the stalls, and is also, in spirit, behind the stage.
Some Experiences of an Irish R.M.

3. To have bought two useless horses in four months was pretty average bad luck. It was also pretty bad luck to have been born a fool.
All on the Irish Shore

4. Perhaps I ought to mention at once that Mr Trinder belongs to the class who are known in Ireland as 'Half-sirs'. You couldn't say he was a gentleman, and he himself wouldn't have tried to say so. But, as a matter of fact, I have seen worse imitations.
All on the Irish Shore

Peter
Somerville-Large

5. How terrible conditions in the North must be if coming to Bray from there was considered to be a holiday.
A Living Dog

6. She had never ceased to have a suspicion that Agnes was not only a Roman Catholic, but had once been a nurse. For her nurses remained unacceptable, sisters of Sarah Gamp.
A Living Dog

7. Drury thought he would never get away. Luckily the television celebrity came into the room. Aware that the eyes of Killiney and Foxrock were upon him, he was sober.
A Living Dog

8. She was a lumpish girl with thick coarse hair that she plaited every day in little plaits and then undid. She had big breasts and dark eyes that managed to look languid and inquiring at the same time, an expression that he had once mistaken for intelligence.
A Living Dog

James
Stephens

9. Cats are a philosophic and thoughtful race, but they do not admit the efficacy of either water

or soap, and yet it is usually conceded that they are cleanly folk.
The Crock of Gold

1. A Leprecaun without a pot of gold is like a rose without perfume, a bird without a wing, or an inside without an outside.
The Crock of Gold

2. In certain ways sleep is useful. It is an excellent way of listening to an opera or seeing pictures on a bioscope. As a medium for day-dreams I know of nothing that can equal it.
The Crock of Gold

3. A thought is a real thing and words are only its raiment, but a thought is as shy as a virgin; unless it is fittingly apparelled we may not look on its shadowy nakedness.
The Crock of Gold

4. All good people like eating. Every person who is hungry is a good person, and every person who is not hungry is a bad person. It is better to be hungry than rich.
The Crock of Gold

5. I never met a thin woman but she was a sour one, and I never met a fat man but he was a fool. Fat women and thin men; it's nature.
The Crock of Gold

6. I know of two great follies – they are love and speech, for when these are given they can never be taken back again, and the person to whom these are given is not any richer, but the giver is made poor and abashed.
The Crock of Gold

7. 'She has tame feet,' said the youth. 'I looked at them and they got frightened.'
The Crock of Gold

8. She could play the piano with such skill that it was difficult to explain why she played it badly.
Desire and Other Stories

9. If once you laugh with a person you admit him to equality.
Desire and Other Stories

10. The winter will come though the lark protest and the worm cries out its woe.
Desire and Other Stories

11. He had married his wife very largely because there was no one else who could so easily be married; and she, after attending quite a respectable time, had married him because no one better had turned up.
Desire and Other Stories

12. The way women have multitudes of feet and stomachs is always astonishing to a child.
Desire and Other Stories

Laurence
Sterne

1. A man's body and his mind, with the utmost reverence to both I speak it, are exactly like a jerkin and a jerkin's lining – rumple the one – you rumple the other.
Tristram Shandy

2. Of all the cants which are canted in this canting world – though the cant of hypocrites may be the worst – the cant of criticism is the most tormenting.
Tristram Shandy

L. A. G.
Strong

3. I was all that lovers prize,
Had my nose not been so long.
O my dears, how cruelly
Half an inch can do us wrong.
Difficult Love

4. Here she sleeps who pleased
    our eyes,
Who was neither good nor wise.
Little weight or worth had she
In our world's community:
Yet in memory she lives on
When the good and wise are gone.
Difficult Love

Jonathan
Swift

5. We have just religion enough to make us hate, but not enough to make us love one another.
Thoughts on Various Subjects

6. Positiveness is a good quality for preachers and orators; because whoever would obtrude his thoughts and reasons upon a multitude, will convince them the more, as he appears convinced himself.
Thoughts on Various Subjects

7. How is it possible to expect that mankind will take advice, when they will not so much as take warning?
Thoughts on Various Subjects

8. No preacher is ever listened to, but time; which gives us the same train and turn of thought, that elder people have tried in vain to put into our heads before.
Thoughts on Various Subjects

9. When we desire or solicit any thing, our minds run wholly on the good side or circumstance of it; when it is obtained, our minds run only on the bad ones.
Thoughts on Various Subjects

10. Religion seems to have grown an infant with age, and requires miracles to nurse it, as it had in its infancy.
Thoughts on Various Subjects

1. All fits of pleasure are balanced by an equal degree of pain, or langour; it is like spending this year, part of next year's revenue.
Thoughts on Various Subjects

2. The latter part of a wise man's life is taken up in curing the follies, prejudices and false opinions he had contracted in the former.
Thoughts on Various Subjects

3. If a writer would know how to behave himself with relation to posterity; let him consider in old books, what he finds, that he is glad to know; and what omissions he most laments.
Thoughts on Various Subjects

4. Whatever the poets pretend, it is plain they give immortality to none but themselves: it is Homer and Virgil we reverence and admire, not Achilles or Aeneas. With historians it is quite the contrary; our thoughts are taken up with the actions, persons and events we read; and we little regard the authors.
Thoughts on Various Subjects

5. When a true genius appears in the world, you may know him by this infallible sign; that the dunces are all in confederacy against him.
Thoughts on Various Subjects

6. Men, who possess all the advantages of life, are in a state where there are many accidents to disorder and discompose, but few to please them.
Thoughts on Various Subjects

7. It is unwise to punish cowards with ignominy; for if they had regarded that they would not have been cowards: death is their proper punishment, because they fear it most.
Thoughts on Various Subjects

8. The greatest inventions were produced in the times of ignorance; as those of the compass, gunpowder and printing; and by the dullest nation, as the Germans.
Thoughts on Various Subjects

9. I am apt to think that in the Day of Judgment there will be a small allowance given to the wise for their want of morals, or to the ignorant for their want of faith; because both are without excuse. This renders the advantages equal of ignorance and knowledge. But some scruples in the wise, and some vices in the ignorant, will perhaps be forgiven upon the strength of temptation to each.
Thoughts on Various Subjects

10. It is pleasant to observe how free the present age is in laying taxes on the next. 'Future ages shall talk of this': 'This shall be famous to all posterity'. Whereas their time and thoughts will be taken up about present things, as ours are now.
Thoughts on Various Subjects

1. It is in disputes as in armies; where the weaker side sets up false lights, and makes a great noise, that the enemy may believe them to be more numerous and strong than they really are.
Thoughts on Various Subjects

2. Some men, under the notions of weeding out prejudices, eradicate religion, virtue and common honesty.
Thoughts on Various Subjects

3. There are but three ways for a man to revenge himself of a censorious world: to despise it; to return the like; or to endeavour to live so as to avoid it. The first of these is usually pretended; the last is almost impossible; the universal practice is for the second.
Thoughts on Various Subjects

4. I have known men possessed of good qualities, which were very serviceable to others, but useless to themselves; like a sun-dial on the front of a house, to inform the neighbours and passengers, but not the owner within.
Thoughts on Various Subjects

5. If a man would register all his opinions upon love, politics, religion, learning and the like; beginning from his youth, and so go onto old age: what a bundle of inconsistencies and contradictions would appear at last.
Thoughts on Various Subjects

6. It is a miserable thing to live in suspense; it is the life of a spider.
Thoughts on Various Subjects

7. The stoical scheme of supplying our wants by lopping off our desires is like cutting off our feet when we want shoes.
Thoughts on Various Subjects

8. The reason why so few marriages are happy is because young ladies spend their time in making nets and not in making cages.
Thoughts on Various Subjects

9. If a man will observe as he walks the streets I believe he will find the merriest countenances in mourning-coaches.
Thoughts on Various Subjects

10. The power of fortune is confest only by the miserable; for the happy impute all their success to prudence or merit.
Thoughts on Various Subjects

11. Ambition often puts men upon doing the meanest office; so climbing is performed in the same posture with creeping.
Thoughts on Various Subjects

12. Censure is the tax a man pays to the public for being eminent.
Thoughts on Various Subjects

13. Satire is reckoned the easiest of all wit; but I take it to be otherwise in very bad times. For it is hard to satirise well a man of

distinguished vices, as to praise well a man of distinguished virtues. It is easy enough to do either to people of moderate characters.
Thoughts on Various Subjects

1. When we are old our friends find it difficult to please us, and are less concerned whether we be pleased or not.
Thoughts on Various Subjects

2. An idle reason lessens the weight of the good ones you gave before.
Thoughts on Various Subjects

3. When the world hath once again begun to use us ill, it afterwards continues the same treatment with less scruple or ceremony; as men do a whore.
Thoughts on Various Subjects

4. Old men view best at distance with the eyes of their understanding as well as with those of nature.
Thoughts on Various Subjects

5. Some people take more care to hide their wisdom than their folly.
Thoughts on Various Subjects

6. Complaint is the largest tribute heaven receives and the sincerest part of our devotion.
Thoughts on Various Subjects

7. The preaching of divines helps to preserve well-inclined men in the course of virtue, but seldom or never reclaims the vicious.
Thoughts on Various Subjects

8. Every man desires to live long, but no man would be old.
Thoughts on Various Subjects

9. Love of flattery in most men proceeds from the mean opinion thay have of themselves: in women from the contrary.
Thoughts on Various Subjects

10. If books and laws continue to increase as they have done for fifty years past, I am in some concern for future ages how any man will be learned or any man a lawyer.
Thoughts on Various Subjects

11. A very little wit is valued in a woman as we are pleased with a few words spoken plain by a parrot.
Thoughts on Various Subjects

12. Old men and comets have been reverenced for the same reason: their long beards and pretences to foretell events.
Thoughts on Various Subjects

13. If a man makes me keep my distance the comfort is he keeps his at the same time.
Thoughts on Various Subjects

14. 'That was excellently observed,' say I, when I read a passage in an author, where his opinion agrees with mine. When

we differ, there I pronounce him to be mistaken.
Thoughts on Various Subjects

1. Every man has just as much vanity as he wants understanding.
Thoughts on Various Subjects

2. A man should never be ashamed to own he has been in the wrong, which is but saying, in other words, that he is wiser today than he was yesterday.
Thoughts on Various Subjects

3. The best way to prove the clearness of our mind is by showing its faults; as when a stream discovers the dirt at the bottom, it convinces us of the transparency and purity of the water.
Thoughts on Various Subjects

4. When men grow virtuous in their old age they only make a sacrifice to God of the Devil's leavings.
Thoughts on Various Subjects

5. The world is a thing we must of necessity either laugh at, or be angry at; if we laugh at it they say we are proud; if we are angry at it they say we are ill-natured.
Thoughts on Various Subjects

6. The greatest advantage I know of being thought a wit by the world is that it gives one the greater freedom of playing the fool.
Thoughts on Various Subjects

7. He who tells a lie is not sensible to how great a task he undertakes, for he must be forced to invent twenty more to maintain that one.
Thoughts on Various Subjects

8. It is with narrow-souled people as with narrow-necked bottles: the less they have in them, the more noise they make in pouring it out.
Thoughts on Various Subjects

9. Many men have been capable of doing a wise thing, more a cunning thing, but very few a generous thing.
Thoughts on Various Subjects

10. Old men, for the most part, are like old Chronicles, that give you dull, but true accounts of times past, and are worth knowing only on that score.
Thoughts on Various Subjects

11. Wit in conversation is only a readiness of thought and facility of expression, or (in the midwives' phrase) a quick conception and an easy delivery.
Thoughts on Various Subjects

12. Human brutes, like other beasts, find snares and poison in the provisions of life, and are allured by their appetite to their destruction.
Thoughts on Various Subjects

1. There is nothing wanting to make all rational and disinterested people in the world of one religion but that they should talk together every day.
Thoughts on Various Subjects

2. Whoever has flattered his friend successfully must at once think himself a knave and his friend a fool.
Thoughts on Various Subjects

3. The same fate hath already attended those other town-wits who furnish us with a great variety of new terms which are annually changed, and those of the last season sunk in oblivion.
An Introduction to Polite Conversation

4. I did then conclude, and still continue to believe, either that wine doth not inspire politeness, or that our sex is not able to support it without the company of women, who never fail to lead us into the right way, and there to keep us.
An Introduction to Polite Conversation

5. I have, likewise, for some reasons of equal weight, been very sparing in double entendres; because they often put ladies upon affected constraints, and affected ignorance.
An Introduction to Polite Conversation

6. A footman can swear; but he cannot swear like a lord.
An Introduction to Polite Conversation

7. Although there seem to be a close resemblance between the two words 'politeness' and 'politicks', yet no ideas are more inconsistent in their natures.
An Introduction to Polite Conversation

8. They failed, as it is generally the case, in too much neglecting to cultivate your mind; without which it is impossible to acquire or preserve the friendship and esteem of a wise man, who soon grows weary of acting the lover, and treating his wife like a mistress, but wants a reasonable companion, and a true friend through every stage of his life.
A Letter to a Young Lady

9. Half a dozen fools are in all conscience as many as you should require; and it will be sufficient for you to see them twice a year.
A Letter to a Young Lady

10. Those who are commonly called learned have lost all manner of credit by their impertinent talkativeness, and conceit of themselves.
A Letter to a Young Lady

1. When you have done a fault, be always pert and insolent, and behave yourself as if you were the injured person; this will immediately put your master or lady off their mettle.
Directions to Servants

2. Never submit to stir a finger in any business but that for which you were particularly hired.
Directions to Servants

3. Providence never intended to make the management of publick affairs a mystery, to be comprehended only by a few persons of sublime genius, of which there seldom are three born in an age.
A Voyage to Lilliput

4. Ingratitude is among them a capital crime, as we read it to have been in some other countries: for they reason thus; that whoever makes ill returns to his benefactor must needs be a common enemy to the rest of mankind, from which they have received no obligation; and therefore such a man is not fit to live.
A Voyage to Lilliput

5. Among people of quality a wife should be always a reasonable and agreeable companion, because she cannot always be young.
A Voyage to Lilliput

John Millington
Synge

6. For these people the outrage to the hearth is the supreme catastrophe. They live here in a world of grey, where there are wild rains and mists every week of the year, and their warm chimney corners, filled with children and young girls, grow into the consciousness of each family in a way it is not easy to understand in more civilised places.
The Aran Islands

7. The outrage to a tomb in China probably gives no greater shock than the outrage to a hearth in Inishmaan gives to the people.
The Aran Islands

8. 'Bedad, then,' he said, 'isn't it a great wonder that you've seen France, and Germany, and the Holy Father, and never seen a man making kelp till you came to Inishmaan.'
The Aran Islands

9. As flannel is cheap – the women spin the yarn from the wool of their own sheep, and it is then woven by a weaver in Kilronan for fourpence a yard – the men seem to wear an indefinite number of waistcoats and woollen drawers one over the other. They are usually surprised at the lightness of my own dress,

and one old man I spoke to for a minute on the pier, when I came ashore, asked me if I was not cold with 'my little clothes'.
The Aran Islands

1. I'd inform again him, but he's burst from Kilmainham and he'd be sure and certain to destroy me. If I wasn't so God-fearing, I'd near have courage to come behind him and run a pike into his side. Oh, it's a hard case to be an orphan and not to have your father that you're used to, and you'd easy kill and make yourself a hero in the sight of it all.
The Playboy of the Western World

2. You never hanged him, the way Jimmy Farrell hanged his dog from the licence, and had it screeching and wriggling three hours at the butt of a string, and himself swearing it was a dead dog, and the peelers swearing it had life.
The Playboy of the Western World

3. It's only with a common week-day kind of murderer them lads would be trusting their carcase, and that man should be a great terror when his temper's roused.
The Playboy of the Western World

4. The peelers is fearing him, and if you'd that lad in the house there isn't one of them would come smelling around if the dog itself were lapping poteen from the dung-pit of the yard.
The Playboy of the Western World

5. There's no sense left on any person in a house where an old woman will be talking for ever.
Riders to the Sea

6. In the big world the old people do be leaving things after them for their sons and children, but in this place it is the young men do be leaving things behind for them that do be old.
Riders to the Sea

Dennis
Taylor

7. Alex [Higgins] is very good at apologising, but then he's had plenty of practice.
Frame by Frame

8. Alex Higgins should have been here today, but he was launching a ship in Belfast and they couldn't get him to let go of the bottle.
Frame by Frame

John (Lord Norbury)
Toler

9. [On being asked to contribute a shilling for the funeral of an impoverished attorney] 'What! Only a shilling to bury an

attorney? Here's a guinea, go and bury twenty-one of them.'
in *John Philpot Curran* by Leslie Hale

Theobald Wolfe
Tone

1. [On a botched attempt to commit suicide in prison by cutting his throat, missing the jugular] I am sorry I have been so bad an anatomist.
in *Theobald Wolfe Tone* by Henry Boylan

William
Trevor

2. Marriage was bound to bring awkwardness; you could not expect otherwise, especially when one of the parties was set in his ways.
The Silence in the Garden

3. A solicitor saw human nature in such miraculous variety, and if there was a single conclusion to be reached it was that in matters governed by human vagaries and weaknesses the law could not be dispensed with.
The Silence in the Garden

4. She'd found him hard to forget at first, not because she'd developed any great fondness for him but because of his nakedness and her own on the hearth-rug,
the first time all that had happened. There hadn't, so far, been a second time.
Office Romances

5. 'Your father came here once or twice, Margaretta, when I was at death's door – called in to offer a second opinion. It wasn't as disagreeable as it sounds, you know, being at death's door. Though nicer, perhaps, to be a few steps further off.'
Virgins

6. Mrs Condon cut slices of loaf bread, and pushed the butter past her husband in Justin's direction. Mr Condon had never been known to pass anyone anything.
Music

7. 'It isn't easy, you know, to marry another man's wife in Ireland.'
The Third Party

8. Cuteness was the one thing you could never get away from in Dubin. Cute weasels they were.
The Third Party

Professor R. Y.
Tyrell

9. 'I shan't vote for X, for he isn't a gentleman and I certainly shan't vote for Samuels, for he is too much of a lady.'
in *The Old Munster Circuit* by Maurice Healy

Mervyn
Wall

1. There was only one refuge in the whole town . . . the National Library; and there he went. He was grateful for the warmth of the reading room, but there was nothing he particularly wanted to read: he had long since grown out of the habit. He was embarrassed by the polite enquiry of the assistant. It was extraordinary: here was an affable young man competent to put a great deal of the world's knowledge before him, and he was unable to think of anything he wanted to know.
A Flutter of Wings

2. The trouble about the overcoat was that he was unable to wear it. He was mortally afraid that a downpour of rain would put it out of shape: it had to hang in the wardrobe in the bedroom until the following month when he could afford to buy an umbrella.
A Flutter of Wings

3. If I had the permission of the owner, my entry on to his land would not constitute a trespass.
A Flutter of Wings

4. He remembered that he had recently read that the manners of policemen always deteriorate under a democratic form of government. It is far better to live under a monarchy if you have dealings with the police.
A Flutter of Wings

5. His mind was so occupied with the shame of being forty years of age that he cut himself twice while he was shaving.
A Flutter of Wings

6. The odour of sanctity was clearly discernible from his breath and person.
The Unfortunate Fursey

7. God's hand was heavy on mankind the day that he created woman.
The Unfortunate Fursey

8. 'Marriage is a folly,' he said sympathetically, 'but it's a respectable one.'
The Return of Fursey

Terence de Vere
White

9. All evening she had been trying to suit her mood to the company, but Irwin's dry little jokes and flirtatious depth-soundings, in the accents of Belfast, which would make even the Song of Solomon sound like a bill of sale, had heightened a longing to be with Alan.
The March Hare

10. Dolly's season had been exciting and anxious; but it had led to no proposals. The very plain son of one of the attorneys upon which her father depended for briefs had been assiduous in calling; but Dolly, nice to

everyone, had given him no exceptional encouragement, and he had never disclosed matrimonial intentions. If he had, she would have considered them. She had a romantic heart but a sober estimate of her attractions.
The March Hare

1. The shy, laughing girl who had aroused his awkward, middle-aged, virgin ardour became in time an overwhelming mate: in this as in all other respects marriage had made her increasingly formidable. After the first two years Dan found that physical love was a short story which he had finished.
Tara

2. In business, on boards, hobnobbing with politicians, kissing bishops' rings, he felt full-up and content; it was at home he felt empty and deflated. In bed his was the state of mind of one who travels on a train without a ticket.
Tara

3. He is a character. Only people who haven't to earn their livings can afford to be characters.
Tara

4. It is impossible for a sensitive person to be present when mixed motives are flying about without being aware of the beating of their wings.
Tara

5. 'Did you know he had translated *Tara* into Irish? He recited it for me. I don't know Irish, but he has such a gorgeous voice he would make a cattle auction sound like the Day of Judgment.'
Tara

6. Mangan came from Cork and O'Connell from Kerry; the inhabitants of neither region can be matched anywhere in the world for circumlocution and evasiveness.
Tara

7. 'Duty! My dear fellow, don't ever do anything as a duty. Duty is what other people want us to do. The dirty work they won't do themselves. I haven't done what you might call my duty for years.'
Tara

W. J. (Jack)
White

8. George was well aware of the Director's views on controversy. He did not, like some men in similar positions, object to his staff shining in public. Their external activities, from reviews in the daily press to papers in the historical journals, he regarded as a form of professional advertising, legitimate and profitable in itself, and conducing to the credit of his own organisation. They tended ultimately to the prime object of the Institute's existence, which,

as with most similar institutions, was that of self-perpetuation.
The Devil You Know

1. . . . the place where they took in the unmarried mothers. Protestants of course.
The Devil You Know

2. Myles used ideas not as toys, like other people, nor as torches to illumine his own path, but as weapons, to be discarded at will when their cutting edge became blunted.
The Devil You Know

3. They were packed in standing among a great many blue-chinned Italians who did not hesitate to enjoy proximity and she was, well, pinched, a sensation she thought about as erotic as a mosquito-bite, and yet it aroused in her an acute awareness that she was a Woman and they Men.
The Devil You Know

4. Unlike so many Irish people, she did not hate her birthplace; nor did she have a strong sentimental attachment to it; it moved her at these moments because it awoke the consciousness of mortality.
The Devil You Know

5. Not many men would want to engage an assistant who had been sued for libelling his last professor . . . I mean, it would be

like marrying a woman who had poisoned her first husband . . .
The Devil You Know

Oscar
Wilde

6. To make a good salad is to be a brilliant diplomatist – the problem is entirely the same in both cases. To know exactly how much oil one must put with one's vinegar.
Vera, or the Nihilists

7. Life is much too important a thing ever to talk seriously about it.
Vera, or the Nihilists

8. We have really everything in common with America nowadays, except, of course, language.
The Canterville Ghost

9. I quite admit that modern novels have many good points. All I insist is that, as a class, they are quite unreadable.
The Decay of Lying

10. No great artist ever sees things as they really are. If he did he would cease to be an artist.
The Decay of Lying

11. Everybody who is incapable of learning has taken to teaching – that is really what our enthusiasm for education has come to.
The Decay of Lying

1. It is exactly because a man cannot do a thing that he is the proper judge of it.
The Critic as Artist

2. The one duty we have to history is to rewrite it.
The Critic as Artist

3. The prig is a very interesting psychological study, and though of all poses a moral pose is the most offensive, still to have a pose at all is something.
The Critic as Artist

4. An idea that is not dangerous is unworthy of being called an idea at all.
The Critic as Artist

5. . . . an unbiased opinion is always absolutely valueless.
The Critic as Artist

6. Education is an admirable thing, but it is well to remember from time to time that nothing that is worth knowing can be taught.
The Critic as Artist

7. The public is wonderfully tolerant. It forgives everything except genius.
The Critic as Artist

8. Learned conversation is either the affectation of the ignorant or the profession of the mentally unemployed.
The Critic as Artist

9. As long as war is regarded as wicked, it will always have its fascination. When it is looked upon as vulgar it will cease to be popular.
The Critic as Artist

10. All bad poetry springs from genuine feelings. To be natural is to be obvious, and to be obvious is to be inartistic.
The Critic as Artist

11. Formerly we used to canonise our heroes. The modern method is to vulgarise them. Cheap editions of great books may be delightful, but cheap editions of great men are absolutely detestable.
The True Function and Value of Criticism

12. Her capacity for family grief is extraordinary. When her third husband died, her hair turned quite gold from grief.
The Picture of Dorian Gray

13. The worst of having a romance of any kind is that it leaves one so unromantic.
The Picture of Dorian Gray

14. I am afraid that women appreciate cruelty, downright cruelty, more than anything else. They have wonderfully primitive instincts. We have emancipated them, but they remain slaves looking for their masters all the same.
The Picture of Dorian Gray

1. Women, as some witty Frenchman once put it, inspire us with the desire to do masterpieces, and always prevent us from carrying them out.
The Picture of Dorian Gray

2. I hate vulgar realism in literature. The man who would call a spade a spade should be compelled to use one. It is the only thing he is fit for.
The Picture of Dorian Gray

3. It is only the shallow people who do not judge by appearances.
The Picture of Dorian Gray

4. It is pure unadulterated country life. They get up early because they have so much to do and go to bed early because they have so little to think about.
The Picture of Dorian Gray

5. He was always late on principle, his principle being that punctuality is the thief of time.
The Picture of Dorian Gray

6. I love acting. It is so much more real than life.
The Picture of Dorian Gray

7. A cigarette is the perfect type of a perfect pleasure. It is exquisite, and it leaves one unsatisfied. What more can you want?
The Picture of Dorian Gray

8. He knew the precise psychological moment when to say nothing.
The Picture of Dorian Gray

9. I can stand brute force, but brute reason is quite unreasonable. There is something unfair about its use. It is hitting below the intellect.
The Picture of Dorian Gray

10. I can't help detesting my relations. I suppose it comes from the fact that none of us can stand other people having the same faults as ourselves.
The Picture of Dorian Gray

11. I am prevented from coming in consequence of a subsequent engagement. I think that would be a rather nice excuse: it would have all the virtue of candour.
The Picture of Dorian Gray

12. There is only one thing in the world worse than being talked about, and that is not being talked about.
The Picture of Dorian Gray

13. Conscience and cowardice are really the same thing. Conscience is the trade name of the firm.
The Picture of Dorian Gray

14. Scepticism is the beginning of Faith.
The Picture of Dorian Gray

15. Those who are faithful know only the trivial side of love: it is the faithless who know love's tragedies.
The Picture of Dorian Gray

16. There is always something ridiculous about the emotions of

people whom one has ceased to love.
The Picture of Dorian Gray

1. The one charm of marriage is that it makes a life of deception absolutely necessary for both parties.
The Picture of Dorian Gray

2. A man can be happy with any woman as long as he does not love her.
The Picture of Dorian Gray

3. Nowadays most people die of a sort of creeping common sense, and discover when it is too late that the only things one never regrets are one's mistakes.
The Picture of Dorian Gray

4. Whenever a man does a thoroughly stupid thing, it is always from the noblest of motives.
The Picture of Dorian Gray

5. I don't want money. It is only people who pay their bills who want that, and I never pay mine.
The Picture of Dorian Gray

6. Young men want to be faithful, and are not; old men want to be faithless, and cannot.
The Picture of Dorian Gray

7. I like Wagner's music better than anybody's. It is so loud that one can talk the whole time without people hearing what one says.
The Picture of Dorian Gray

8. One should never make one's *debut* with a scandal. One should reserve that to give an interest to one's old age.
The Picture of Dorian Gray

9. The longer I live the more keenly I feel that whatever was good enough for our parents is not good enough for us.
The Picture of Dorian Gray

10. I should think that the real tragedy of the poor is that they can afford nothing but self-denial.
The Picture of Dorian Gray

11. The public have an insatiable curiosity to know everything. Except what is worth knowing. Journalism, conscious of this, and having tradesman-like habits, supplies their demands.
The Soul of Man under Socialism

12. With regard to modern journalists, they always apologise to one in private for what they have written against one in public.
The Soul of Man under Socialism

13. A true artist takes no notice whatever of the public. The public to him are non-existent. He leaves that to the popular novelist.
The Soul of Man under Socialism

14. We have been able to have fine poetry in England because the public do not read it, and consequently do not influence it. The public like to insult poets

because they are individual, but once they have insulted them, they leave them alone.
The Soul of Man under Socialism

1. There is only one class in the community that thinks more about money than the rich, and that is the poor. The poor can think of nothing else.
The Soul of Man under Socialism

2. Agitators are a set of interfering meddling people, who come down to some perfectly contented class of the community and sow the seeds of discontent among them. That is the reason why agitators are so absolutely necessary.
The Soul of Man under Socialism

3. One of Nature's gentlemen, the worst type of gentlemen I know.
Lady Windermere's Fan

4. I don't like compliments, and I don't see why a man should think he is pleasing a woman enormously when he says to her a whole heap of things he doesn't mean.
Lady Windermere's Fan

5. I like talking to a brick wall; it's the only thing in the world that never contradicts me.
Lady Windermere's Fan

6. A man who moralises is usually a hypocrite, and a woman who moralises is invariably plain.
Lady Windermere's Fan

7. Between men and women there is no friendship possible. There is passion, enmity, worship, love, but no friendship.
Lady Windermere's Fan

8. How marriage ruins a man. It's as demoralising as cigarettes, and far more expensive.
Lady Windermere's Fan

9. It's most dangerous nowadays for a husband to pay any attention to his wife in public. It always makes people think that he beats her when they're alone.
Lady Windermere's Fan

10. There's nothing in the world like the devotion of a married woman. It's a thing no married man knows anything about.
Lady Windermere's Fan

11. London is too full of fogs – and serious people. Whether the fogs produce the serious people or whether the serious people produce the fogs, I don't know, but the whole thing rather gets on my nerves.
Lady Windermere's Fan

12. Illness of any kind is hardly a thing to be encouraged in others. Health is the primary duty of life.
Lady Windermere's Fan

13. In this world there are only two tragedies. One is not getting what one wants and the other is getting it.
Lady Windermere's Fan

1. One should never trust a woman who tells one her real age. A woman who would tell one that, would tell one anything.
A Woman of No Importance

2. The history of women is the history of the worst form of tyranny the world has ever known. The tyranny of the weak over the strong. It is the only tyranny that lasts.
A Woman of No Importance

3. Men marry because they are tired; women because they are curious. Both are disappointed.
A Woman of No Importance

4. We women adore failures. They lean on us.
A Woman of No Importance

5. LORD ILLINGWORTH: . . . a title is really rather a nuisance in these democratic days. As George Hartford I had everything I wanted. Now I have merely everything that other people want, which isn't nearly so pleasant.
A Woman of No Importance

6. The Peerage is one book a young man about town should know thoroughly and it is the best thing in fiction the English have ever done.
A Woman of No Importance

7. There is a good deal to be said for blushing, if one can do it at the proper time.
A Woman of No Importance

8. All Americans lecture . . . I suppose it is something in their climate.
A Woman of No Importance

9. Duty is what one expects from others, it is not what one does oneself.
A Woman of No Importance

10. It is perfectly monstrous the way people go about, nowadays, saying things against one behind one's back that are absolutely and entirely true.
A Woman of No Importance

11. Nothing spoils a romance so much as a sense of humour in the woman – or the lack of it in a man.
A Woman of No Importance

12. The English country gentleman galloping after a fox – the unspeakable in full pursuit of the uneatable.
A Woman of No Importance

13. A really *grand passion* is comparatively rare nowadays. It is the privilege of people who have nothing to do. That is the one use of the idle classes in a country.
A Woman of No Importance

14. Men are horribly tedious when they are good husbands, and abominably conceited when they are not.
A Woman of No Importance

1. Memory in a woman is the beginning of dowdiness.
A Woman of No Importance

2. Music always makes one feel so romantic – at least it always got on one's nerves – which is the same thing nowadays.
A Woman of No Importance

3. To win back my youth . . . there is nothing I wouldn't do – except take exercise, get up early, or be a useful member of the community.
A Woman of No Importance

4. He must be quite respectable. One has never heard his name before in the whole course of one's life, which speaks volumes for a man, nowadays.
A Woman of No Importance

5. Moderation is a fatal thing. Nothing succeeds like excess.
A Woman of No Importance

6. To love oneself is the beginning of a life-long romance.
Phrases and Philosophies for the Use of the Young

7. The old believe everything; the middle-aged suspect everything; the young know everything.
Phrases and Philosophies for the Use of the Young

8. Any preoccupation with ideas of what is right or wrong in conduct shows an arrested intellectual development.
Phrases and Philosophies for the Use of the Young

9. Wickedness is a myth invented by good people to account for the curious attractiveness of others.
Phrases and Philosophies for the Use of the Young

10. Ambition is the last refuge of the failure.
Phrases and Philosophies for the Use of the Young

11. The only way to atone for being occasionally a little over-dressed is by being always absolutely over-educated.
Phrases and Philosophies for the Use of the Young

12. I always pass on good advice. It is the only thing to do with it. It is never any use to oneself.
An Ideal Husband

13. He has one of those terribly weak natures that are not susceptible to influence.
An Ideal Husband

14. Women have a wonderful instinct about things. They can discover everything except the obvious.
An Ideal Husband

15. Extraordinary thing about the lower classes in England – they are always losing their relations. They are extremely fortunate in that respect.
An Ideal Husband

1. . . . when the Gods wish to punish us they answer our prayers.
An Ideal Husband

2. Once a week is quite enough to propose to anyone, and it should always be done in a manner that attracts some attention.
An Ideal Husband

3. One should never give a woman anything she can't wear in the evening.
An Ideal Husband

4. Morality is simply the attitude we adopt to people whom we personally dislike.
An Ideal Husband

5. Musical people are so absurdly unreasonable. They always want one to be perfectly dumb at the very moment when one is longing to be absolutely deaf.
An Ideal Husband

6. Women are never disarmed by compliments. Men always are. That is the difference between the sexes.
An Ideal Husband

7. Only people who look dull ever get into the House of Commons, and only people who are dull ever succeed there.
An Ideal Husband

8. I don't at all like knowing what people say of me behind my back.

It makes one far too conceited.
An Ideal Husband

9. Philanthropy seems to have become simply the refuge of people who wish to annoy their fellow creatures.
An Ideal Husband

10. Fashion is what one wears oneself. What is unfashionable is what other people wear.
An Ideal Husband

11. Fathers should neither be seen nor heard. That is the only proper basis for family life.
An Ideal Husband

12. She wore far too much rouge last night and not quite enough clothes. That is always a sign of despair in a woman.
An Ideal Husband

13. Bachelors are not fashionable any more. They are a damaged lot. Too much is known about them.
An Ideal Husband

14. To be natural is such a very difficult pose to keep up.
An Ideal Husband

15. Thirty-five is a very attractive age. London society is full of women of the very highest birth who have, of their own free choice, remained thirty-five for years.
The Importance of Being Earnest

1. The only way to behave to a woman is to make love to her, if she is pretty, and to someone else, if she is plain.
The Importance of Being Earnest

2. The truth is rarely pure and never simple. Modern life would be very tedious if it were either, and modern literature a complete impossibility.
The Importance of Being Earnest

3. The very essence of romance is uncertainty. If ever I get married, I'll certainly try to forget the fact.
The Importance of Being Earnest

4. Relations are a tedious pack of people, who haven't got the remotest knowledge of how to live, nor the smallest instinct about when to die.
The Importance of Being Earnest

5. All women become like their mothers. That is their tragedy. No man does. That is his.
The Importance of Being Earnest

6. Few parents nowadays pay any regard to what their children say to them. The old-fashioned respect for the young is fast dying.
The Importance of Being Earnest

7. To lose one parent . . . may be regarded as misfortune; to lose both looks like carelessness.
The Importance of Being Earnest

8. Good looks are a snare that every sensible man would like to be caught in.
The Importance of Being Earnest

9. The amount of women in London who flirt with their own husbands is perfectly scandalous. It looks so bad. It is simply washing one's clean linen in public.
The Importance of Being Earnest

10. In England, at any rate, education produces no effect whatsoever. If it did, it would prove a serious danger to the upper classes, and would probably lead to acts of violence in Grosvenor Square.
The Importance of Being Earnest

11. I never travel without my diary. One should always have something sensational to read in the train.
The Importance of Being Earnest

12. I dislike arguments of any kind. They are always vulgar, and often convincing.
The Importance of Being Earnest

13. All charming people, I fancy, are spoiled. It is the secret of their attraction.
The Portrait of Mr W. H.

14. A thing is not necessarily true because a man dies for it.
The Portrait of Mr W. H.

Jack B.
Yeats

1. He loved the wild and open spaces. 'I love them wild, and if they aren't wild, I'll wild them.'
The Charmed Life

2. Opposite the meal-house is an extraordinary thing – an empty public-house! Decayed, its licence gone long ago; its lamp glassless and twisted. Its walls, whose pillars once shone painted marble, now show a smeared blue and green that makes the passer-by think of fogs and deep-sea moans. The windows were boarded up in an age gone. The place would be full of rats if there was anything left to eat there. Even rats won't nest in a derelict gold mine because of the name.
The Charmed Life

3. Bowsie, I say, out of nothing, you would never make a clerk in a bank, you have not got the necessary gloss. Did you notice how glossy those were this morning? I don't mean their clothes – some of them were wearing a sort of half sporting jacket. I mean about their heads. Smoothed out, in round figures. All figures should be rounded towards you and me. Ten thousand pounds are far, and away, better than nine hundred and ninety-nine pounds, nineteen shillings and eleven pence.
The Charmed Life

4. One windy night I saw a fisherman staggering, very drunk, about Howth Pier and shouting at somebody that he was no gentleman because he had not been educated at Trinity College, Dublin. Had he been an Englishman he would have made his definition of 'gentleman' depend on money, and if he had been not only an Englishman, but a Cockney, on the excellence of the dinner he supposed his enemy to have eaten that day. My drunken fisherman had a profound respect for the things of the mind, and yet it is highly probable that he had never read a book in his life, and that even the newspapers were almost unknown to him. He is only too typical of Ireland. The people of Ireland respect letters and read nothing. They hold the words 'poet' and 'thinker' honourable, yet buy no books.
The Charmed Life

5. He takes up now a fashion magazine. A cover design that might have come from the studio of a designer, who was ready to follow Picasso – if he was let.
The Charmed Life

6. Sea-gulls have the gift of changing their shape, and size, at will. One type of gull will in an hour look as all types.
The Charmed Life

1. I have never seen snow. I was never on a winter day in the land when snow was on the ground. Snow doesn't like me. It melts before I come.
The Charmed Life

2. If he knew that he had wrung a Judge's heart it would lie no heavier than a feather of the ceannbán lies on the bog.
The Charmed Life

3. Another thing they couldn't understand was the want of blaspheming and cursing in the printed page.
The Charmed Life

4. A robin that isn't a robin red-breast, looks like a bank messenger in mufti.
The Charmed Life

5. Nowadays we've altered most of those Aesop's fables. The pot, if it is to boil ever, requires constant watching.
The Charmed Life

6. A multi-millionaire now can hardly get a shave without paying the barber a percentage on his income. And disguising himself in rags, and pretending to be poor, has only had the result of making every poor tramp on the roads suspected of being a hidden millionaire. So the millionaire, without doing himself any good, has harmed others.
The Charmed Life

7. If you dine out of tins, you should have the labels served up, with the grub.
The Charmed Life

8. I wonder when a sea-gull turns his beak into his chest, and fixes his view, is he looking in his ignorance, in the wrong place for his navel. And of course he never had one.
The Charmed Life

W. B. Yeats

9. We poets would die of loneliness but for women, and we choose our men friends that we may have somebody to talk about women with.
in *Irish Literary Portraits* by W. R. Rodgers

10. Do you know it is possible to be a senior wrangler and yet have only the most common place idias? What poor delusiveness is all this 'higher education of women'. Men have set up a great mill, called examinations, to destroy the imagination. Why should women go through it, circumstance does not drive *them*. They come out with no repose, no peacefulness – their minds no longer quiet gardens full of secluded paths and

umbrage circled nooks, but loud as chaffering market places.
Letters, 1865 – 1895

1. [To R. M. Smyllie, who had just told him he had won the 1923 Nobel Prize for Literature] And tell me, Bertie, how much is it worth?
from *Mr Smyllie, Sir* by Tony Gray

2. The only trouble with Seamus O'Sullivan is that when he's not drunk he's sober.
in *My Father's Son* by Frank O'Connor

3. [To a Duke who asked him at a London party whether or not he supported W. T. Cosgrave] Oh no, I support the gunmen – on both sides.
in *My Father's Son* by Frank O'Connor

(Michael Moran)
Zozimus

4. O long life to the man who
     invented potheen –
Sure the Pope ought to make him
     a martyr –
If myself was this moment
     Victoria, our Queen,
I'd drink nothing but whiskey and
     wather.
In Praise of Potheen

5. Saint Patrick was a gintleman,
     he came of decent people,
In Dublin town he built a church,
     and upon't put a steeple;
His father was a Callaghan, his
     mother was a Brady,
His aunt was an O'Shaughnessy,
     his uncle was a Grady.
Saint Patrick was a Gintleman

Index of Subjects

Index of Key and Cogent Words and Phrases